Y0-EFS-283

THE RESURGENCE OF RIGHT-WING RADICALISM IN GERMANY

THE RESURGENCE OF RIGHT-WING RADICALISM IN GERMANY

New Forms of an Old Phenomenon?

Edited by
ULRICH WANK

Translated by
James Knowlton

HUMANITIES PRESS
NEW JERSEY

Originally published in German as *Der neue alte Rechtsradikalismus*
© R. Piper GmbH & Co., KG, München, 1993

This English translation first published in 1996 by
Humanities Press International, Inc. 165 First Avenue,
Atlantic Highlands, New Jersey 07716

English translation © 1996 by Humanities Press International, Inc.

Library of Congress Cataloging-in-Publication Data

Der neuer alte Rechtsradikalismus. English
    The resurgence of right-wing radicalism in Germany : new forms of
an old phenomenon? / edited by Ulrich Wank; translated by James Knowlton.
      p. cm.
    Translation of Der neue alte Rechtsradikalismus, R. Piper GmbH & Co.,
KG, München, 1993.
    Includes index.
    ISBN 0-391-03958-X. —ISBN 0-391-03959-8 (pbk.)
    1. Fascism—Germany—History—20th century. 2. Antisemitism-Germany—
History—20th century. 3. Germany—Politics and government—20th century. I.
Wank, Ulrich. II. Title.
JN3972.A91N49 1996   95-42978
                                                     CIP

Printed in the United States of America

CONTENTS

FOREWORD

When Fritz Rene Allemann's book *Bonn ist nicht Weimar* [*Bonn Is Not Weimar*] appeared in 1955, the title quickly became a slogan, even a platitude. Compared to the first German republic, the history of the Federal Republic reads like a success story: Undergirded by the *Wirtschaftswunder*, the economic miracle of the fifties, the new nation quickly established a political stability the likes of which were unknown in the Weimar Republic. Levels of affirmation of the state and its constitution were high, parliamentary majorities were comfortable, and extremist parties played as good as no role at all. In retrospect it is easy to forget that in these years, too, there was a series of political struggles and crises—not to mention deficiencies, such as the failure to deal fully with the Nazi past. "Fair-weather democracy," too, had to seek a mooring gradually in the consciousness of the Germans. However, there is no doubt that this has succeeded.

This positive image of Germany has lost much of its glitter in recent years. Politics and politicians are in the middle of a crisis of confidence, the causes of which lie deeper than the larger and smaller scandals of 1992–93. Symptomatic of this is the fact that the cohesive force of the large popular parties is in decline. If we count the percentages of the popular vote the large parties CDU/CSU and SPD have received, we note that in 1976 they reached a high with 91.2 percent. Since 1976, these numbers have declined steadily until in the last federal election of 1992 the parties achieved only a total of 77.3 percent: "The popular parties are losing the populace" (Heribert Prantl). A parallel to this development is the rise of the proportion of eligible voters who do not vote. Where in 1976 the number of nonvoters was 9.3 percent, by 1990 it had risen to 22.7 percent.

In this situation it is a matter of great concern that—for the first time since the episodic rise of the NPD between 1964 and 1969—right-wing radicalism is on the increase in Germany. The "pressure from the right" (Claus Leggewie) is growing. Doubts about parliamentary democracy, exaggerated nationalism, and hatred of foreigners, coupled with anti-Semitism, have become an explosive mixture that has acquired new volatility from the economic recession and a vague fear of the future. Even more remarkable is that what in the past had been limited to beery talk in pubs has now become political action: a network of rightist associations, parties, activist groups,

vii

and newspapers has established a foothold. From these circles emanate what are euphemistically called "violent excesses" and "xenophobic unrest"—and political murder by the right.

Just in the past year (1992), seventeen people were killed by right-wing radicals in attacks on domiciles for foreigners, riots, or attacks on individuals. No matter how closely linked we take right-wing groups to be, it is clear that in recent years an atmosphere of right-wing violence has arisen. "The murders in Solingen and Mölln are not unrelated, individual crimes. They stem from a climate created by the right-wing scene. Even individual criminals do not appear from nowhere" (Richard von Weizsäcker).

When in 1972 the Red Army Faction began its terrorist activities, Heinrich Böll spoke of the "struggle of the six against sixty million." With this phrase he accurately described the complete isolation of these terrorists from the rest of society. But there is reason to fear that this is not the case today.

In an attempt to counter this political climate, publisher Ernst Reinhard Piper in 1993 initiated a lecture series on the topic "The Resurgence of Right-Wing Radicalism in Germany: New Forms of an Old Phenomenon?" The papers presented in the series are collected in this book.

The intention was to portray right-wing radicalism in its historical continuity. Particularly when discussing this topic in Germany, the past always has to be considered and pondered: to what degree does the current right-wing radicalism take up themes from the rightist German tradition (such as anti-Semitism); to what extent does it represent a new development?

Maintaining the series' historical intentions, the first essay of the book treats anti-Semitism and anti-Judaism in German history. *Julius H. Schoeps* traces the transformation of Christian anti-Judaism to racially determined anti-Semitism and describes the character of anti-Jewish attitudes throughout German intellectual history—all the way to the paradoxical situation of an anti-Semitism that makes do without Jews.

Ernst Piper documents and analyzes the rise of the Nazi movement after World War I. He discusses the movement's cross-connections all the way into Munich's "high society," which forcefully supported Hitler, and demonstrates how the movement, using nationalist and rightist elements, shaped an ideology whose aura of fascination reached all the way into Munich's middle class.

In 1933 the National Socialists succeeded in eliminating the first German democracy. *Peter Longerich* demonstrates that the fall of the Weimar Republic was not predestined and that this democracy was indeed capable of defending itself from the rightist assault. He separates the success story of the Nazi Party from the failure of the Weimar Republic and treats the Nazi seizure of power in the light of three key questions: How did a Nazi mass movement arise? How was Hitler appointed chancellor of the Reich? How was the Hitler government able to establish a dictatorship?

Otto Schily examines the perils to which the second German democracy was exposed in the sixties. He not only considers the NPD, which has remained little more than a footnote in the history of the Federal Republic, but also the German susceptibility to antidemocratic and totalitarian ideas in this period.

"In today's rampant right-wing radicalism we are not dealing with a force from the German past but with something essentially new: a product of postwar modernism." This is the thesis of *Thomas Schmid*, who deals with right-wing radicalism in a unified Germany. He considers whether the recent welling up of right-wing radicalism is associated with unification and to what extent it is a classical right-wing extremist movement.

The book concludes with an essay by *Bassam Tibi*, who closes the circle that took shape at the beginning of the book and who compares xenophobia with hostility toward Jews. To ward off xenophobia—and with it right-wing radicalism—Tibi demands an active integrationist policy from both sides involved: Germans should be prepared to integrate the foreigners living in Germany, and the foreigners for their part should be willing to accept the values of the democratic West: democracy, tolerance, and the separation of religion and politics. He illustrates his argument with the example of Islam and Islamic fundamentalism.

Right-wing radicalism will continue to play a role in the now expanded Federal Republic of Germany. A return to the almost idyllic conditions of the old Federal Republic seems almost inconceivable. "Bonn was not Weimar. But Berlin is also not Bonn," as Claus Leggewie has put it. What will become of this new republic will in no small part depend on how effectively we succeed in countering the resurrected spirit of right-wing radicalism. This book would like to be understood as a contribution to this process.

—Ulrich Wank

1

FROM ANTI-JUDAISM TO ANTI-SEMITISM: ON THE STRUCTURE, FUNCTION, AND EFFECT OF A PREJUDICE

JULIUS H. SCHOEPS

The relationship of Jews to other peoples is largely determined by the trauma of Auschwitz. The Holocaust left deep scars not only in the thinking and feeling of Jews. The destruction of European Jewry, the mass murder of the Jews of Europe, tolerated and even abetted by the silence of the rest of the world, still makes itself felt and will continue to influence Jews and non-Jews in the future. The fear of a return of this horror, the fear that this inconceivable event could again become reality, is omnipresent. This fear cannot be easily brushed aside, particularly because so many aspects of the Holocaust have yet to be explained. How was it possible that a cultured nation in the heart of Europe slipped into barbarism? Was it merely a logical consequence of the biological foundation of a racist ideology that had been elevated to a kind of racial mythology? Or was it simply due to the insane ideas of a madman who led his subalterns of all ranks and social classes to the point where they would commit murder on a mass-production scale?

One thing is certain: since the destruction of the temple in A.D. 70, since the period of the banishment and Diaspora, the problem between the Jews and other peoples has existed—the problem of a minority whose members maintained their identity via religion, tradition, and history—this despite the fact that differences developed in terms of religion, customs, and culture

1

and that the Jews readily adapted to the conditions in the countries in which they resided. In his commendable study *The Jewish Question: Biography of a Worldwide Problem*, Jerusalem historian Alex Bein, who died in 1988, presented the view that it was "most likely the Jews themselves who had created the preconditions for the existence of the so-called Jewish question."[1] They did not cease to exist as a people; they managed to maintain their identity, and to a certain degree they refused to accept the "rules of the game" of the peoples where they lived. Despite the complete collapse of their identity as a nation-state and of their religious center, despite the so apparent demonstration of their own powerlessness and the powerlessness of their God, they held fast to their religion and the way of life that arose from it. But, Bein argues, it was presumably just this attitude that led to the misunderstanding with which many non-Jews have not been able to come to grips even until today.

There is no doubt that there were always times in which people encountered the Jews in a positive way, but the normal case was rejection. Anyone who is looking for a real answer to the question of what in the last analysis is behind the rejection of the Jews must have the courage to pose questions that are as radical as possible. Hostility toward Jews as a phenomenon cannot be comprehended if we only examine and interpret it from the outside. Hatred of the Jews always has to do with oneself, with one's own self. For this reason it is quite difficult to take a hard, honest look at this topic. It remains a constant irritant. When we honestly seek to get to the bottom of these questions we become troubled by a sense that our own identity might be challenged. And that is something that few people desire and that most people fear.

It would be a great mistake to consider anti-Semitism, as the hatred of the Jews is known in its modern incarnation, to be solely and exclusively a reaction to crises in capitalist society. This is an interpretation that is modern but that in the last analysis offers few insights and remains too shallow to do justice to the phenomenon. Hatred of the Jews has, and this is the crux of what I will argue here, its roots in religious convictions, particularly in the difference between Christians and Jews—in the traditional rejection of Jews by Christianity and the Christian world.

1. HATRED OF THE JEWS AS A CONSEQUENCE OF CHRISTIAN INDOCTRINATION

The conception that the Jews have been cursed and abandoned by God because they failed to recognize Jesus as the Messiah and were responsible for his crucifixion—this notion has determined the Christian image of the Jews through the centuries and continues to determine it today. Even after 1945 we find the argument in the "Word on the Jewish Question" by the

Fraternal Council of the Evangelical Church of Germany: "By crucifying the Messiah, Israel relinquished its status as the chosen and elect."[2]

Not social reality but the accusations of the church fathers from Origines through Augustine and John Chrystostomos all the way to Jerome created the stereotype, the distorted image of the Jews that has been handed down from generation to generation. Repeatedly recast as the archetypal figure of the sinner and blasphemer, the Jew serves as a forbidding example. With the catechism, children and adults absorb this image in church via sermons. Every church sculpture and every church painting about the passion and crucifixion of the Savior and the martyrs reminds the viewer of this. In songs, tales, and even in passion plays—this image is omnipresent. It is an image that bundles the anti-Jewish prejudices that have been in circulation for eons; it also (and I am aware of the controversial nature of this statement) contains an indirect appeal to the viewer to break with the Jews and to resist them with violence if necessary.

The accusation of murdering God, formulated in various parts of the New Testament, has maintained its presence over the centuries and has determined Christian attitudes toward the Jews. There is no anti-Jewish argument "that has been used longer, brought forth more persistently, been more doggedly maintained, or more deeply internalized" (Stefan Lehr). The accusation of murdering God has precipitated feelings of hatred, generated prejudices, and persistently poisoned the relationship between Christians and Jews. Repeated as a stereotype through the centuries, this accusation has managed to stylize the Jew in popular consciousness as a demon and caused him to assume the features of an Ahasver, of a restless wanderer through the world. One came to see in him the blood-sucking vampire, the goat-hoofed devil, the Satan with a tail—he became the personification of all calamity, the incarnation of evil.

The image of the outcast and thus depraved Jew created by the church fathers is the foundation for all later hostility and persecution. This image acquired its particular shape through the feelings of estrangement that Jews have caused in non-Jews until today. On the one hand, this is doubtless a function of the religious-ethnic isolation of the Jews, who since antiquity have met with mistrust and rejection; on the other hand, it is related to the Jews' persistent faith in the singularity of an invisible God and in particular to their claim to be the chosen people—a claim that others until today have viewed as arrogant superstition, as godlessness, and even as deceit.

The Christian world's rejection of the Jews' claim to be a chosen people is epitomized in a very early Jewish self-definition in the person of a jesting Midrash who employs the following play on words: On Mt. Sinai sin came down upon the peoples of the earth ["Am Sinai sei die sina [sin] auf die Völker der Welt herabgestiegen"]. By this is meant that the election of the

Jews to receive the Torah is accompanied by the jealousy, hate, and rage of the peoples of the world who were not chosen. This is no doubt a strong and concrete reason for hostility toward the Jews: the belief that God made a covenant with Abraham and his successors, a covenant that Moses renewed on Mt. Sinai and by which Israel was predestined to be the chosen people of God and to become an instrument to bless mankind.

For over two thousand years people have done everything in their power "to adapt the real image of the Jews to the one that was propagated by the church" (Alex Bein). The Christian world perceived the existence of Jewry as irksome, as intolerable. Even a Protestant theologian as important as Karl Barth was not able to free himself from a feeling of distaste. Once he remarked in a letter to Friedrich Wilhelm Marquard that when he met Jews he was always forced to suppress a "completely irrational aversion."[3]

In the last analysis it is always the same image that has been passed along over the centuries: the Jew as "Anti-Christ" who must be opposed in order to secure one's own sense of self. The means that church princes and politicians thought up to achieve this resemble each other in a strange way. Even though centuries separate them, there is a remarkable resemblance in the laws of the Lateran Council, the Spanish laws of the sixteenth century, and the Nuremberg Laws of the Nazis ("Laws to Protect German Blood and German Honor" of 15 September 1935). It is readily apparent that certain notions about how it would be possible to isolate the Jews have been maintained through the centuries.[4]

Thus, for example, the prohibition of marriage between Jews and Christians of 1935 is only different in wording ("marriages between Jews and German citizens or people of related blood are prohibited") from earlier versions. The prohibition of using servants in Jewish households, which was promulgated in 1215, was rephrased in 1935 in the following way: "Jews are prohibited from employing female German citizens or people of related blood under forty-five years of age in their households."[5]

Even the yellow star that was pinned to the Jews for the purpose of marking them was not an invention of the Nazis but a part of an old church tradition. The Lateran Council decreed that Jews were to be made identifiable by using special clothing or markings. This policy of specially marking Jews had as its goal to distinguish Jews from the rest of the population in Christian lands; it was taken up by the Nazis and used as a means both to mark and to humiliate Jews. We can only speculate how they "chose" yellow. Probably they knew—as zealous consumers of German culture, perhaps from Goethe's Theory of Colors—that this color has long carried negative connotations. In any case they surely knew this color had been used since time immemorial to mark banished people such as whores, heretics, and desecrators of the Host—and also Jews.

2. SECULAR IMAGES OF JEWS AND FEAR OF THE JEWISH PERIL

With the end of the eighteenth and the beginning of the nineteenth century a new development began that was to become a deadly threat for the Jews. Emancipation brought them step by step toward equality, but it failed to secure them the desired social recognition for which they struggled with every ounce of their being. On the contrary, the more rights they obtained and the more they adapted themselves to the clothing, speech, gestures, and behavior of the surrounding society, the greater was the malignancy of the rejection they experienced. Rabid anti-Semites developed strategies to isolate the Jews—strategies that were aimed not only at reversing the emancipation process but also at making the Jews increasingly visible as a group. "Every Jew that one sees," wrote Edouard Drumont, "every Jew who openly shows himself for what he is, is relatively less dangerous. . . . The Jew who is unrecognizable—that is the dangerous Jew."[6]

But how can one recognize someone who cannot be visibly distinguished from other people? Are there ways to achieve visual distinction? Anti-Semites made a sport of marking Jews by their names. In the study *The Name as Stigma*, written by Cologne linguist and culture scholar Dietz Bering, one can read about the sophisticated tricks that were employed here.[7] In the Weimar Republic there were countless jokes, verses, and satirical songs in which a Jewish-sounding name such as Cohn, Hirsch, or Katz was made the target of derision and scorn (an example: "Über allen Gipfeln Ozon; unter allen Wipfeln sitzt Kohn" [Over all hilltops ozone; under the treetops sits Cohn]—a paraphrase of the first lines of a well-known poem by Goethe).

Josef Goebbels, Nazi propaganda minister, was a true virtuoso in using names as a weapon—for example, in his relentless attacks on Berlin chief of police Bernhard Weiß, whom he titled "Isidore"—to stoke up anti-Semitism in the population.[8] Goebbels knew instinctively that his attacks hit the location that is constitutive with all people: names have much to do with most people's identity, and a directed attack on a name is a way to destroy the name-holder's personality—a practice that was systematically conducted during the Weimar Republic to stigmatize the Jews and to prepare their segregation from society.

The chief motivating factor for the isolation and segregation campaigns of the last century was apparently deep-seated fear of Jews—fear that stemmed from the accelerating modernization processes that caused large social upheavals and that also affected the individual. In addition to this, the churches and thus also the Christian religion increasingly not only lost ground in the nineteenth century but also relinquished a measure of persuasive power. The place of traditional religion was gradually assumed by a rational system of beliefs and scientific thought, which for reformers came to be the main alternative. But this did not apply to the broad mass of society, which felt threatened by the fact that the once so stable social order was in flux and that images and concepts that had been valid for centuries were now perceived to be obsolete.

In the course of the transition from feudal to bourgeois-capitalist society an increasing number of people had difficulty finding balance in their emotional and spiritual lives. All sorts of things were made responsible for this, and this had a definite effect on the Jews, of whom it was believed that they were they real people behind all these contradictory and threatening things. The pogroms of 1819, which entered history as the so-called Hep-Hep Riots, did not break out without warning. They had been prepared in speech and print by intellectuals such as Fichte and the long-since-forgotten but at the time enormously influential university professors Jakob Friedrich Fries and Christian Friedrich Ruehs, who were notorious enemies of the Jews.

People eagerly snapped up anti-Semitic slogans such as those from the extreme anti-Semite Hartwig von Hundt-Radowsky, who called himself "the second Grattenauer." His *Judenspiegel* that appeared in Würzburg in 1819 contained a clearly pornographic-aggressive undertone and suggested that Jewish girls be put in bordellos and that Jewish men be castrated and forced to work in mines or sold to the English, who could sell them to their overseas colonies as slaves. Hundt-Radowsky's demand to exterminate the Jews or at least to drive them out of Germany represented a qualitatively new stage of hostility toward the Jews—a stage that must be seen as an early form of more modern anti-Semitic annihilation strategies.

In this context it is important to note whether and to what extent traditional Christian religious convictions and remnants of Christian theology became amalgamated with apparently nonreligious phenomena of the nineteenth century. German nationalism, which had arisen during the French Revolution and in the course of the subsequent Wars of Liberation, embodies the liberal idea of self-determination and the democratic idea of national sovereignty while at the same time displaying a thinly veiled redemptive strain, which was evident in the conviction that Christianity was a German religion and that liberation would emanate from Germanized Christianity or Christianized Germanity.

The new Romantic conception of the people that stemmed from Herder and Fichte, the patriotic sermons of Ernst Moritz Arndt ("Einmüthigkeit der Herzen sey eure Kirche, Haß gegen die Franzosen eure Religion, Freyheit und Vaterland seyen die Heiligen, bei welchen ihr anbetet" [unanimity in your hearts should be your church, hatred of the French your religion; freedom and fatherland should be the saints you worship]), and the notion that the German people were the primal, unadulterated "blessed people" (Jahn) are signs for this Christian missionary spirit and the consciousness of the redemptive power of the German people. These then are the structural elements that have become integral parts of German nationalism.

Thus it was only a small step to transforming the traditional theological antithesis Jewry–Christianity into the antithesis Jewry–Germanity [*Deutschtum*]. The traditional image of the Jew, the stereotype of the demonic anti-Christian Jew, was thus transformed—or modernized—at the end of the eighteenth and the beginning of the nineteenth centuries. The Jew was now no longer the Anti-Christ, the damned one; now he became the usurer, the speculator, the price inflator, the financial manipulator, the archenemy, a danger for the economic and political existence of Germany and of the Germans.

Christian hostility toward the Jews was at the beginning of the modern period aimed at defaming or isolating Jews, not at annihilating them. The Jews were seen as having been cursed by God, condemned to servitude, and scattered around the world. But they were always able to release themselves from the divine curse by accepting baptism and converting to Christianity. The racial theories that arose in the beginning of the nineteenth century left no such way out. God's religious curse and banishment of the Jews were replaced by the topos of the Jew having an inalterable racial character that was defined as inferior. Thus the Jew was no longer a vague concept. Instead, he became a "corporeal reality, a fixed human character, determined by race and definable in his traits" (A. Bein).

In addition to the German-nationalist patriots such as Jahn and Arndt, the so-called scholarly critique of religion [*wissenschaftliche Religionskritik*] made major contributions to establishing anti-Semitic racial theories. This critique was aimed at religion in general but especially at the Jews and Jewry. Left-Hegelian Bruno Bauer, for example, was a definite opponent of the Jews, and in the course of his career he became a doctrinaire teacher of German conservatism and a supporter of abstruse racial theories. Bauer was one of the first in Germany to speak of "racial types" and to confirm the existence of racial traits [*Raceneigentümlichkeit*] and desired to establish a clear demarcation line between Jews and non-Jews. "Baptism," Bauer once noted, "cannot make a Jew a German."[9]

The image of the Jew that had been sketched out by the enemies of the Jews was doubtless a mirror image of the time and the consciousness that produced it. One attacked the Jews but also vaguely comprehended that this was also an attack on one's own way of thinking, an attack on humanity itself. But it became increasingly clear that Christianity was losing influence over everyday life. At the same time, it was clear that people were willing and eager to hold fast to the explanatory models offered by the church and that traditional hostile images were still capable of influencing their behavior. The text of a broadside from the Viennese Revolution of 1848 makes it plain that people were clearly conscious of how contradictory this was. This text is remarkably prophetic in that it suggests what the Jews can expect from a world that has lost its faith: "The Christians who no longer have Christian faith will become the most fearsome enemies of the Jews. . . . When the Christians no longer have Christianity nor money . . . then, you Jews, have steel skulls made for yourselves, for with skulls made of bone you will never survive history."[10]

3. REDEMPTION AND ANNIHILATION

The transition from a religious hostility toward to Jews to modern anti-Semitism can be illustrated very well with the case of Richard Wagner. Wagner, who understood his musical and printed works as a unity [Gesamtkunstwerk], was a Jew-hater whose thought was produced by a mixture of religious and racial motives. For him it was no longer a matter of isolating the Jews; he wanted them annihilated. In Das Judentum in der Musik [Jewry in Music], his polemical work of 1850, Wagner had not only denied Jews any talent for musical creativity but also characterized them as parasites, as dark and demonic, and as burdened with the Ahasverian curse. "But just think," wrote Wagner in the last sentence of his pamphlet, "that only one thing can redeem you from the curse you bear: the redemption of Ahasver—your destruction!"[11]

With his Parzival, which was conceived as a Bühnenweihfestspiel [stage consecration festival], Wagner presented to the world not only the idea of the "Aryan Christ" but also a dark vision of the "destruction of the world" [Weltvernichtung], of the Welt-Aufhebung [the abolition of the world] that was to precede the return of Christ. Wagner and his followers were convinced that the self-annihilation of the Jews would have to precede the awakening of the Germans. In endlessly new variations, Wagner occupied himself with this theme that has been suppressed and even disputed by many a contemporary Wagnerian.

Richard Wagner's "redemptive theories" not only influenced the middle-class culture of Wilhelminian Germany but also contributed to a large extent to the formation of the racist worldview that in the last analysis erupted in the "final solution of the Jewish question." Munich literary scholar Hartmut Zelinsky has demonstrated in a revealing documentation and in numerous essays how Hitler and the Nazis co-opted Wagner's work and misused it for propagandistic purposes.[12] One of the many demonstrations for this is a statement by August Kubizek, Hitler's boyhood friend, who in his memoirs, which he published after 1945, stated that Hitler "sought in Wagner more than just a model and an example. I can only say: he appropriated the personality of

Wagner; he set out to acquire Wagner so completely that this man could become a part of his own being."[13]

Anyone who is willing to make the effort of comparing Hitler's notes before the Munich putsch and his confessional book *Mein Kampf* with Wagner's *Mein Leben* [*My Life*] will note how seriously Hitler relied on central Wagnerian concepts such as rebirth, purity, maintaining the purity of blood, mixing blood, goddess of want, signs for the degeneration of mankind, world-moving idea, Germanic revolution, or Germanic state. Entire passages about Jews and anti-Semitism, says Harmut Zelinsky, appear to be Wagner paraphrases, which make it clear how much Hitler saw in Wagner not only a genius but also the prophet of his pan-Germanic dreams and his anti-Jewish mania.

The secret of the success Hitler and the Nazis enjoyed with the Germans was most likely that the folkish ideology they propagated had a Christian-religious core. People felt directly affected by Nazi propaganda and the Nazi's semiliturgical acts (celebrations for the martyrs of the movement, marches in Nuremburg, the creation of "German hallowed places" [*Weihestätten*]. They believed that Hitler understood them and that in National Socialism they were members of something akin to a church. The view is gaining currency that Hitler's National Socialism was a genuine cultic-religious movement, a movement that had appropriated all the mythological functions of a religion. Absolute adherence to the doctrine and total subjugation were required. From the beginning, Hitler cast himself in the role of the redeemer-leader [*erlösender Führer*] (probably so long that he believed it himself) and enjoyed being celebrated as the "Messiah of all Germans."

In the speeches and texts by Hitler and his followers one can find numerous passages of a Gnostic and apocalyptic nature. We read of good and evil, light and darkness. The Jewish demon stands in opposition to the Aryan man of light. We find the topos of the Third Reich and allusions to the Apocalypse of John. In *Mein Kampf* we can read: "Thus today I believe that I am acting in accordance with the almighty creator: by opposing the Jews I am fighting for the work of the Lord."[14] One cannot prove any more clearly than with these words how much Christianity and National Socialism had entered into a quasi-symbiotic relationship. With the formulation "By opposing the Jews I am fighting for the work of our Lord," Hitler established an identification with the role of the savior and redeemer—with the figure who would free Germans from affliction and lead them to the light.

A large part of the population fell for this fusion of religion and politics in National Socialism—as did numerous Christian theologians. New Testament scholar and Bonn University professor Ethelbert Stauffer, for example, demanded that all devout Christians also be National Socialists. His New Testament scholar-friend at the University of Tübingen, Gerhard Kittel, argued in much the same vein. One of the spokesmen of the "German Christians," Kittel, like many other renowned theologians in the years after 1933, justified the Nazis' segregation policy and placed himself squarely behind the Nazi policy on Jews.[15] This resulted from his conviction that Christianity was in its very essence anti-Jewish; thus every honest Christian should feel obliged to support the Nazi policy on Jews in word and deed.

Increasingly, anti-Jewish stereotypes had their effect on the language before and after 1933. Considering that language reflects concepts and thoughts but also that language can determine the consciousness and modes of thought for an entire epoch, it is important for our context to take note of the words and verbal images that theologians, politicians, literary people, and publicists have used over the centuries. Particularly since the second half of the nineteenth century, people have characterized Jews as "parasites" that "degenerate" and "poison" the "body of the folk." One can read of "bacilli" and "trichinas," of "rats" and "blowflies." Popular in the Nazi period and still in current use today is the image of the "parasite"; it suggests that the Jew lives at the cost of other people, that he uses flattery and submissiveness to garner advantages without generating real productive labor.

Hitler and his followers had internalized the image of the "parasite." In the Jews they saw a parasitic race that can only survive at the cost of "hosts" and by exploiting other peoples and races. At the Nuremberg Party Congress in 1937, Goebbels, borrowing Wagner's formulations, summarized the various images and conceptions of the Jew in the following words: "Behold, this is the enemy of the world, the destroyer of cultures, the parasite among the peoples of the world, the son of chaos, the incarnation of evil, the real, visible demon of the degeneration of mankind."[16]

It is certain that these verbal images and conceptions, stemming from the arsenal of biology, contributed to weakening the last moral restraints, the inner resistance against injustice and crime, in millions of people. Presumably this image of the Jew, as Alex Bein assumes, contributed to no small extent to the methods of organized murder of the Jews. Just as in the Middle Ages one killed Satan and the Anti-Christ with the Jew, the method of gassing in Hitler's murderous camps represents the logical consequence once the image of the Jew as a parasite had finally become established. If the Jews really were bacilli and parasites and vermin, then it was not only imperative to exterminate them—it was also necessary to do so with the means with which one eradicates bacilli and vermin: poisonous gas.

4. ANTI-SEMITISM WITHOUT JEWS

After 1945 people in Germany believed for a long time that anti-Semitism had been overcome. Until the early seventies people were convinced that knowledge about the organized mass murder had cleansed the Germans, had exerted a quasi-cathartic effect. That may have been so in individual cases. This and that person perhaps really did know nothing of the entire extent of these horrors. On the other hand, it is today impossible to maintain the ritualized assertions that people were simply not informed about what had happened to the Jews. This assertion was and is a popular argumentational figure used for general exculpation; but it has the side effect that it serves to conceal feelings of guilt and bad conscience.

Anti-Semitic prejudices are still present. Empirical studies by social scientists demonstrate that 15 percent of the population of the Federal Republic is openly anti-Semitic and that an additional 30 percent is latently anti-Semitic.[17] The remarkable thing about these statistics is not so much the numbers themselves as the fact that anti-Semitism does not require living Jews for its articulation. A right-wing skinhead who hollers "Out with the Jews" and sprays anti-Semitic slogans on gravestones in Jewish cemeteries as a rule knows neither Jews nor anything about Judaism. But that does not prevent him from understanding himself as an anti-Semite.

Anti-Semitism appears to have a psychosocial function. A population confronted with a problem of some kind still needs a scapegoat as a kind of psychic release valve. That was no different in the past than it is now—with the one difference that there are no longer any living Jews on whom pent-up feelings of jealousy, hate, and frustration can be vented. Concepts like "Jew" and "Jewry" have assumed an independent existence. In a sense they have become metaphors of evil. Skinheads use them consciously or unconsciously, as do honorable politicians, particularly when they feel helpless in certain situations and are convinced that a guilty party must be found for their plight.

In post-Holocaust German society, Jews, numerically speaking, hardly play a role. Despite that, the aversion toward them is still quite deeply rooted. Responsible for this is doubtlessly the centuries-old caricatured image that, burned into the consciousness of most people, no longer needs real Jews to take effect. Anti-Semitism leads an indeterminate life of its own. Already in 1816 Ludwig Börne stated that the aversion to Jews arose from "a congenital fear of ghosts" and had its roots in the magical-mythical conceptual world of the Christian population.[18] Similarly, Odessa physician Leon Pinsker, who diagnosed anti-Semitism as a kind of "fear of ghosts," argued sixty years later that anti-Semitism was a kind of congenital neurosis that was not accessible to rational argumentation and was incurable.[19]

This free-floating image of the Jew, this anti-Jewish prejudice without (concrete) Jews, stands at the end of a development that began with hatred of the murderers of God. Anti-Judaism has been transformed into anti-Semitism and has remained influential in Germany to this day.

Can we do anything about this? It is certainly not enough to schedule an annual "Brotherhood Week," which has become a ritualized event of which the public hardly takes notice. Films, books, and plays, too, which are more likely to reflect culture than influence such matters, hardly change these constellations of consciousness. A dyed-in-the-wool anti-Semite does not suddenly stop being an anti-Semite just because he is ordered to do so. After all, why should he? Any psychoanalyst can confirm that anti-Semites are quite satisfied with their prejudice. They do not wish to be rid of it, nor are they accessible to attempts to enlighten them.

Anti-Semitism cannot be affected by the usual means of enlightenment. Perhaps a conceivable possibility would lie in retheologizing the Christian-Jewish relationship. This would mean that Christians would continue rethinking their disturbed relationship to the Jews. A number of things along this line have happened in recent years. There are exemplary synodal resolutions and Protestant council declarations that give reason for hope but that also demonstrate the limits of theological efforts. The 1980 synodal resolution of the Protestant church in the Rhineland ("we acknowledge the responsibility and the guilt of Christianity in Germany for the Holocaust") met with resistance from professors of the theological faculty of the University of Bonn, for whom the eight-point declaration went too far and who thus felt compelled to express their opposition.[20]

The needed inner-Christian renewal process will only lead to the desired goal if Protestants and Catholics are not afraid to reconsider the self-definition of Christianity. And herein lies the real problem. If one is to strike anti-Judaism from church documents, then one would have to do without missions to the Jews and would even have to confess the Christian responsibility for the suffering of the Jews—at which point one would be justified in asking whether this new Christianity has anything to do with the original version. These renewal efforts have caused a number of clergy and laypeople to feel that their faith and their identity are being challenged; they thus have vehemently refused to accept the proposed changes in the Christian-Jewish relationship.

It could be that the struggle against anti-Semitism is a hopeless task. Historical experience dictates that might well be the case. But even if we accept hopelessness we should continue to accept our obligation to humanitarian ideals and tolerance and to make an effort to resist prejudice wherever we find it. The recognition that there are limits to what we can achieve is a bitter truth, but that should not prevent us from making ourselves felt wherever injustice occurs and prejudice militantly determines people's thoughts and deeds. An inalterable precondition for this to have a chance of success, however, would be radical enlightenment efforts and real motivation—in families, in religious instruction, at school, in the lecture halls of universities, and even at the workplace. Can anything be achieved? The answer is not certain. But we have no other choice.

NOTES

1. On the Jewish question cf. Alex Bein, *Die Judenfrage. Zur Biographie eines Weltproblems* (Stuttgart, 1980), 1:3ff.
2. Printed in Gerhard Czermak, *Christen gegen Juden. Geschichte einer Verfolgung* (Nördlingen, 1989), 259f.
3. Karl Barth to Friedrich Wilhelm Marquardt, 5 September 1967, in *Karl Barth, Briefe 1961–1968* (Karl Barth, *Gesamtausgabe*, vol. 5), ed. Jürgen Fangmeier and Heinrich Stoevesandt (Zurich, 1975), 420–21.
4. There is hardly an anti-Semitic measure that does not have a precise model in church history. Cf. Raoul Hilberg's table in which canonical and Nazi anti-Semitic measures are compared (*Die Vernichtung der europäischen Juden* [Berlin, 1982], 15f).
5. *Verfolgung, Vertreibung, Vernichtung. Dokumente des faschistischen Antisemitismus 1933–1942* (Leipzig, 1983), 113.
6. Edouard Drumont, *La France juive* (Paris, 1943), 1:322.
7. Dietz Bering, *Der Name als Stigma. Antisemitismus im deutschen Alltag 1812–1933* (Stuttgart, 1987).
8. Cf. Dietz Bering, *Kampf um Namen. Bernhard Weiß gegen Joseph Goebbels* (Stuttgart, 1991), 229ff.
9. Bruno Bauer, in Hermann Wagener, *Staats- und Gesellschaftslexikon*, 23 vols. (Berlin, 1859–67), 7:12.
10. Broadside of 1848, Vienna, Stadtbibliothek E 50395.
11. Richard Wagner, *Gesammelte Schriften und Dichtungen* (Leipzig, 1911), 5:85.
12. See in particular the "'Plenipotentarius des Untergangs' oder der Herrschaftsanspruch der antisemitischen Kunstreligion des selbsternannten Bayreuther Erlösers Richard Wagner. Anmerkungen zu Cosima Wagners Tagebüchern 1869–1883," *Neohelicon* (Budapest and Amsterdam, 1982), 9:145–76; *Richard Wagner. Ein deutsches Trauma. Eine Dokumentation zur Wirkungsgeschichte Richard Wagners 1876–1976* (Berlin and Vienna, 1983); "Richard Wagners 'Kunstwerk der Zukunft' und seine Idee der Vernichtung," *Von kommenden Zeiten. Geschichtsprophetien im 19. und 20. Jahrhundert*, ed. Joachim H. Knoll and Julius H. Schoeps (Stuttgart and Bonn, 1983), 84–106; "Das erschreckende 'Erwachen' und wie man Wunder von Hitler befreit," *Neue Zeitschrift für Musik* (September 1983): 9–16; "Die deutsche Losung Siegfried oder 'innere Notwendigkeit' des Judenfluchs im Werk Richard Wagners," *In den Trümmern der eigenen Welt—Richard Wagners Der Ring der Nibelungen*, ed. Udo Bermbach (Hamburg, 1989), 201–49.
13. August Kuslek, *Adolf Hitler, mein Jugendfreund* (Graz and Stuttgart, 1953), 84.
14. Adolf Hitler, *Mein Kampf* (Munich, 1926), 70.
15. Cf. Leonore Siegele-Wenschkewitz, "Protestantische Universitätstheologie in der Zeit des Nationalsozialismus," *Antisemitismus*, ed. Günter Brakelmann and Martin Rosewski (Göttingen, 1989), 52–76.
16. Cf. Bein (see note 1), 1:361.
17. Cf. Alphons Silbermann, *Sind wir Antisemiten? Ausmaß und Wirkung eines sozialen Vorurteils in der Bundesrepublik Deutschland* (Cologne, 1982); also *Antisemitismus*

nach dem Holocaust. Bestandsaufnahme und Erscheinungsformen in deutschsprachigen Ländern, ed. Alphons Silbermann and Julius H. Schoeps (Cologne, 1986).

18. Ludwig Börne, *Sämtliche Schriften*, ed. Inge and Peter Rippmann (Dreieich, 1977), 1:137.

19. Cf. Julius H. Schoeps and Leon Pinsker, "'Autoemanzipation!'—Ein Mahnruf von 1882," *Beter und Rebellen, Aus 1000 Jahren Judentum in Polen*, ed. Michael Brocke (Frankfurt, 1983), 223–35.

20. Rolf Rendtorff and Hans H. Henrix, *Die Kirchen und das Judentum. Dokumente 1945–1985* (Paderborn and Munich, 1988), Document E 11129.

2

THE FALL OF THE WEIMAR REPUBLIC AND THE NATIONAL SOCIALIST SEIZURE OF POWER

PETER LONGERICH

1. AFTER THE UNIFICATION OF GERMANY: NEW INSIGHTS AND PERSPECTIVES

On 1 July 1933, almost exactly sixty years ago, police officers in the Berlin homicide squad were called to the district of Köpenick, where two bodies had been pulled from the Dahme River, a tributary of the Spree. Both had been tied into sacks that had been weighted down with paving stones. Both bodies displayed, in addition to gunshot wounds, signs of having been tortured.

Within a few days the police succeeded in determining the identity of the two murder victims. One of them was a Paul von Essen, a functionary of the *Reichsbanner Schwarz-Rot-Gold* [Reich Banner Black-Red-Gold] group; the other was the previous Social Democratic minister president of Mecklenburg, Johannes von Stelling. Both had been reported missing since 21 June after they had been kidnapped by SA men.

In the next few days police received further reports of bodies in Köpenick. There were two men who had been brought to the hospital with serious injuries and had died of poison. An additional four bodies were found in the Dahme. More bodies had been buried in hastily shoveled graves in the surrounding woods.

All these dead people were victims of an unprecedented massacre by the Berlin SA, who in the course of a week had kidnapped and tortured hundreds of people in Köpenick, mostly Social Democrats and Communists. In addition to the deaths, numerous cases of serious injury were reported, and many of the victims had been bestially disfigured.

These crimes, which became known as the "Bloody Week of Köpenick," represented at that point the largest complex of related crimes that had been committed during the "National Socialist seizure of power." It is assumed that twenty-one people lost their lives. The Bloody Week of Köpenick marks the climax and the conclusion of the violent Nazi coup d'état. The brutal excesses of Köpenick demonstrated to party and government leaders that SA terror, if it was to continue, could take on unsuspected dimensions. Much speaks for the idea that the events in Köpenick led the Nazi leadership to declare the so-called end of the National Socialist revolution in July of 1933, an attempt to control the open terrorism of the SA in favor of police state methods.

Among the victims of Köpenick was Johannes von Stelling, an important figure in Weimar democracy. As minister president, member of the SPD party board of directors, and member of the "directorium," the last leadership committee of the Social Democrats in the Reich, von Stelling was one of the top Social Democratic politicians to fall victim to Nazi terror between 1933 and 1945.

It is remarkable that this leading politician of the Weimar SPD, who was brutally tortured and murdered, has been completely forgotten in the Federal Republic. Not only that: The events in Köpenick, which have been described in detail in the relevant literature, have by and large been neglected.

In contrast to the old Federal Republic, East Germany constantly emphasized the murders in Köpenick, which was part of East Berlin, by creating a memorial, organizing memorial celebrations, by brochures, treatment in schools, etc., thus elevating the Köpenick events to a symbol of antifascist resistance. But no detailed scholarly investigation of the Köpenick events was ever conducted in East Germany.

The fact that the Bloody Week of Köpenick was largely ignored in the West and subjected to ostentatious and ritualized treatment in the East is related to the trial that was conducted in the summer of 1950 at the state court in East Berlin against sixty-one ex-SA men and that concluded with fifteen death sentences. This trial, conducted at the height of the Cold War, was used by East Germany to attack the West. Half of the defendants were tried in absentia—they were living comfortably in the West. In the West, the trial was largely ignored or debunked as a show trial. This defensive attitude led to the most brutal Nazi massacre of 1933 being forgotten.[1]

The example of the Bloody Week of Köpenick clearly demonstrates that the unification of 1989–90 can have a great effect on our historical struggle to grasp the Nazi past. The end of the Cold War opened previously closed archives in the old eastern bloc, and this has enriched our understanding of the Nazi period by adding important facts; it has permitted us to develop historical insights that had been impossible before.

The end of the Cold War and the restoration of the German national state have opened up new perspectives on the Nazi state. In 1993 there are many good reasons to reexamine 1933. The now larger German state is awakening, by virtue of its size, new fears that the German tradition of seeking to attain great power status might be reawakened. Germany's foreign policy initiatives are being met in their initial phases with historically motivated distrust. The end of the postwar order has influenced the new version of the old right-wing radicalism like a stroke of liberation. Whether it can grow to become a mass movement is no longer a question that can be ignored; it must be taken seriously. In the united Germany the wish to create a new German identity is obstructed by the year 1933.

The thought that intensive attempts to come to grips with the past [*Vergangenheitsbewältigung*] might lead to putting Nazism behind us has proven to be illusory. We see that within German history the preoccupation with the causes and effects of 1933 will take a central position in the long term. The year 1933 marks the point at which German history deviates from the developmental lines of modern Western democracy.

The fact that this period of German history is repeatedly placed in the foreground irritates many people who see this threatening the status and integrity of the nation. Recently such thoughts were heard in this country on the occasion of the opening of the Washington Holocaust Museum. But these people are overlooking the fact that studying the Nazi period is not what is causing negative light to be cast on the image of Germany; it is, rather, the events of this period themselves that are having such a damning effect.

When commentators speak in an offended tone about the "Americanization" of Holocaust memory, they are lamenting a co-optation of Nazi history that is only possible because there is no comparable national effort—nor will there be one soon—to build a central site to memorialize, study, and research the Nazi period. The Nazi dictatorship represents such a massive incursion into other people's history that the rest of the world must occupy itself with this period whether we do so or not. Our only choice is to decide to what extent we want to participate in the ongoing discussion about our own past.

If it is true that each epoch writes its own history anew, then the epoch-making transformation of 1989 should motivate us to increase our efforts, to produce an inventory of research about the Nazi period, and to at least partially revise our understanding of this period.

But this is not only a question of collecting more historical facts and

closing gaps. The entire regional and local history of the Nazi period in the
East German states is still virgin terrain. Our understanding of the local
character of National Socialism is basically limited to the west of Germany.
Opening archives that were not accessible means, to take an example for
important tasks facing research on the Nazi past, explaining the great number
of known disposition and situation reports that were produced by the various offices in the Third Reich. If we were to compare and evaluate these
documents, we would be able to place our poor understanding of the mental
history and the mood and attitudes of people in the Third Reich on a new
footing.[2]

But the main concern is, as I suggested before, shifting our perspective
after the end of the Cold War. Such a change could emerge not only from
the growing temporal distance to National Socialism but also and in particular from that fact that a completed epoch, which we might call the postwar period, lies between the Nazi period and today.[3] That has a variety of
consequences. The Nazi dictatorship, which can now be surveyed as the
history of its consequences, can now also be grasped as possessing a deeper
historical dimension. Instrumentalizing the horrors of National Socialism for
the ideological struggle between the two blocs is now a thing of the past—
unless we want to fight this battle anew. Historical comparisons will help
answer the question whether there is an essential relationship between the
Communist and Nazi dictatorships or whether both systems are fundamentally distinct. Categorizing National Socialism in the German and European
history of the twentieth century will, in the last analysis, be the goal of
research work that has been made fruitful by such new perspectives.

At the outset of this kind of new beginning must stand the demand to
develop a new set of concepts—concepts that are relevant to the Nazi period. To describe and depict many events of this time we still use the language of the National Socialists. Repeatedly employing this vocabulary and
blithely putting it in quotation marks can only be a contingent solution.
Concepts are elementary to our understanding a different epoch.

Thus when we deal with 1933 we frequently use the contemporary terms
"seizure of power" or "National Socialist revolution," which are products of
Nazi manipulation of the language.[4] These terms evoke the notion of a he-
roic uprising that, as we shall see, never happened.

2. WAS THE NAZI TAKEOVER INEVITABLE?

We have arrived at our actual topic. The Nazi takeover, as I will call it,
reached its climax and its end with the massacre in the summer of 1933.
With it, the foundation was laid for a dictatorship that encompassed virtu-
ally every aspect of life.

Only five years before, in 1928, the Weimar Republic found itself at a peak of a seemingly promising development. The democratic parties had emerged from the Reichstag elections with new strength. The domestic climate had been pacified; the danger of a putsch by the right seemed to have been averted in the long run. The economy was about to reach its prewar standard again. Unemployment was being kept within manageable limits. Freedom and mass culture were flourishing.

In the light of this dramatic transformation within only five years, the causal question poses itself with all the greater urgency.

One can quickly produce a plethora of arguments for the fall of the Republic and the Nazi takeover—for example, the worldwide depression, the failure of democratic forces, mistakes in the constitution, the antidemocratic attitude of the elites, the consequences of World War I. We could even go back farther and seek reasons in authoritarian-statist traditions or the relatively minor political participation of the middle class, whereby our grasp of the period would take on greater depth but would also begin to get blurry around the edges.

Several years ago one of the leading researchers on the Weimar Republic, Hagen Schulze, collected all these possible causes in a catalogue that totaled more than 120 points.[5] Detailed literature exists on each of these points, and because of this great thematic scope, historians of Weimar have long since gone over to organizing themselves in specialized scholarly groups, such that we now have specialized research on parties, organizations, elections, inflation, and local aspects of the Nazi period.

The problem, then, is less finding arguments for the fall of the Weimar Republic than assessing and weighing these various factors and trying to present explanatory models in a comprehensive form.

In the light of the multitude of potential causes that could explain the fall of the Weimar Republic it would be a good idea to link all the causes together in a scenario and declare the fall of the Weimar Republic and the rise of National Socialism to be inevitable. But we gain little using this argument of inevitability. If we assume the fall of the Weimar Republic to have been inevitable we can only conclude that what happened had to happen the way it happened. The end of Weimar would then appear to be a consequence predestined by historical necessity. What we need, however, are historical *explanations*. We should strive to make clear which options were present and for which reasons certain alternatives were able to assert themselves or to fail.

In examining the causes of 1933 we should carefully distinguish between the success story of the NSDAP and the weakness of Weimar democracy. Furthermore, there exists the problem that what generated Hitler can be adequately explained neither by the lowered resistance of democracy nor by the acts of Nazi leadership. If we were to limit our scenario to these two factors, then we would have to deny autonomy to all the mass movements that supported National Socialism, and we would not be able to assess the role the leadership elites played in transforming the Weimar state into a Nazi dictatorship.

I think we can most productively shed light on the causes for the take-over by answering three questions:

How was it possible for the Nazi mass movement to arise?

How was Hitler named chancellor of the Reich?

How was it possible for the Hitler government to implement a dictatorship?

I would like to elucidate these questions from the end, i.e., from the per-spective of the summer of 1933.

3. IMPLEMENTING A DICTATORSHIP

The first question I would like to discuss is thus the transformation of Hit-ler's chancellorship to a dictatorship. With Hitler's appointment as Reich chancellor on 30 January 1933, which took place within the framework of the Weimar constitution, there still existed no Nazi dictatorship. Implement-ing a dictatorship depended upon a series of circumstances: The National Socialists first had to violently eliminate their opponents, and they had to suspend the constitution. They were only able to achieve these things be-cause their conservative partners in government assented and because the apparatus of the state, i.e., military, bureaucracy, justice, and police, was prepared to support and execute National Socialist policies. Thus the trans-formation of the chancellorship to a dictatorship is only an inevitability for those who consider these preconditions to be given and who are not pre-pared to continue to problematize them.

Yet setting up the dictatorship between January and June of 1933 oc-curred as a multistage process.

The first step in expanding the power base of the National Socialists was to dissolve the Reichstag, in which the Hitler government did not possess a majority. This was a step that Hindenburg, despite reservations by conservative members of the government, was prepared to take. The election campaign that began then once again offered the NSDAP the opportunity to mobilize its propaganda apparatus to its full extent. The election campaign of the parties on the left was kept in check by terror by the SS and SA, who were now working with government support.

Thanks to the Emergency Law that had been passed on 4 February 1933, the government not only had at its disposal the option of outlawing newspa-pers and assembly, it also had, thanks to Göring's appointment as commissioner in the Prussian ministry of the interior, the majority of the police apparatus in its hands.

Not only were police officers willing to look the other way when SA and SS attacked opponents—Göring had also urged them in a decree "to make ruthless use of firearms." Five days later Göring decreed that the police force was to be expanded by around fifty thousand auxiliary officers, most of whom were recruited from the SA, the SS, and the Stahlhelm [a right-wing veterans' association].

The burning of the Reichstag in the night of 27 to 28 February 1933 provided the needed pretext for the new government to aggressively expand its power base: The National Socialists portrayed the fire as a Communist revolt and used it to destroy what was left of the Communist apparatus and to arrest members of parliament and leading functionaries of the Communist Party.

With the Decree for the Protection of People and State [Verordnung zum Schutz von Volk und Staat] that was issued the day after the burning of the Reichstag, the basic rights of the Weimar constitution were suspended. At the height of the election campaign, the government now had at its disposal an unlimited instrument of power.

In the elections of 5 March 1933 there were many cases of people being prevented from voting and other electoral irregularities. In spite of this, the National Socialists only managed to garner 43.9 percent of the votes. However, the governing coalition of the Nazis and the Deutschnationale Volkspartei [German National People's Party], which received 8 percent of the votes, acquired a parliamentary majority.

Thus the first phase of the takeover was concluded. Hitler had availed himself of all his opportunities to expand his power base by promulgating an extreme interpretation of the Emergency Law.

The second phase included eliminating all opponents and neutralizing the remaining political and social institutions. At first the new rulers went after the parties of the left, then the Jewish minority, the middle-class faction, and government institutions, in the end not even sparing their coalition partners, the German Nationals.

The next step after the elections of 5 March was to neutralize the states and communities in an attempt to implement the National Socialist claim to total power. Here, too, the decree that followed the burning of the Reichstag offered the decisive leverage. It permitted the federal government to intervene if state governments were not able to secure public order. Nazi tactics now consisted of creating such allegedly unmanageable unrest with the help of their own followers. The government of the Reich then appointed Reich commissars in the states. The Bavarian government, which was the last state government to yield its independence, fell in mid-March.

The end of the states' independent political role was then sealed by two laws "zur Gleichschaltung der Länder mit dem Reich" [Laws for the Purpose of Bringing the States into Line with the Reich]. The states were now under control of Reich governors [*Reichstatthalter*].

In many towns and cities a similar process took place. The following pattern is discernible: At first the National Socialists marched to the city hall and demanded that the swastika flag be raised. If the municipal officials refused, then the Nazi supporters would implement their will using massive force. In many cases, mayors were violently forced to resign.

The second step on the way to the Nazi dictatorship was to concentrate state power in the Reich government. An enabling law that changed the constitution was to place the government in a position to independently decree laws, even laws that did not conform with the constitution. In this way the parliament was to be eliminated and the independence of the Reich president broken.

By eliminating the eighty-one Communist members of parliament it was possible to substantially reduce the size of the quorum needed to change the constitution. But since the needed number of NSDAP and German National votes could not be attained, several votes from the middle-class faction were still required. For this purpose Hitler secured support of the center by verbally assenting to a number of changes in the constitution and in church policy. But he never produced the promised written confirmation of the agreement. After long discussions the smaller parties of the middle also decided to support the proposed bill. Only the forty-nine Social Democratic representatives present rejected the Enabling Law.

March also saw an increase in the number of attacks on Jews by Nazi supporters. The Nazi leadership now decided to link the wave of "spontaneous" protests to an organized act. For 1 April 1933 they planned a boycott of all Jewish businesses. This was intended to bring the excesses under control while sending a signal that economic discrimination against the Jews was a goal of government policy. A few days later several discriminatory special laws aimed at the Jews were passed. An example is the Law to Restore a Professional Civil Service [Gesetz zur Wiederherstellung des Berufsbeamtentums] that removed Jews and supporters of the democratic parties from civil service.

In addition to neutralizing the states and attacking the Jews, the National Socialists began in March to concentrate their attacks on the Social Democrats and the trade unions; in our chronology this is the fourth step on the road to establishing a dictatorship. Numerous offices and newspaper presses were also occupied and destroyed. The unions tried to break their close political link to the SPD and even supported transforming 1 May, the traditional day to celebrate the working-class movement, into a legal holiday, which would be called the "day of national labor." But these celebrations, conducted with great propagandistic extravagance as a way of symbolizing the new National Socialist "ethnic community" [*Volksgemeinschaft*], were in reality the prelude to eliminating unions altogether. The day after the holiday, 2 May, all union facilities were occupied and the unions were forced to merge with the National Socialist "German Labor Front."

The Social Democrats, whose organization was still fundamentally intact but was being rapidly weakened, tried to assert themselves. Gradually it became clear that the SPD had lost the basis from which it would conduct its political work. In the beginning of May the SPD board of directors decided that important members of the party leadership should go abroad. A few days later the total assets of the SPD and its newspaper were confiscated. On 21 June the Reich minister of the interior decreed a prohibition of all party activities.

A further wave of neutralization measures broke over the system of associations in the spring and early summer of 1933. Retail associations, the handworkers' associations and guilds as well as those of industry and trade, and the entire system of agricultural associations and chambers were forced into National Socialist–dominated organizations. Industry countered the Nazi demands for neutralization by creating a Reich League of German Industry [Reichsstand der Deutschen Industrie] and by replacing the leadership positions at the top of its professional associations. By setting up an Adolf Hitler Charity of German Business [Adolf-Hitler-Spende der deutschen Wirtschaft] the practice of irregular charitable contributions by industry was replaced by a constantly growing fund that was at Hitler's personal disposal.

This wave of neutralizations, however, did not exhaust itself on business associations but extended to the entire system of clubs and private associations, from sports associations to choral clubs and all the way to amateur gardener clubs. The goal of this policy was to bring all types of organizations under the control of the Nazi movement.

To round out the picture one must also mention the waves of neutralizations and purges with the help of which the new rulers brought the entire cultural life and all branches of public opinion under its control. They began massively after the creation of the propaganda ministry by Goebbels in March 1933 and reached their height with the book burnings in May.

Finally, in May and June of 1933, the last of these assault waves hit the right-wing conservative allies of the National Socialists. Now even the public meetings of the DNVP were interfered with. Here, too, there was violence. The Stahlhelm organization now saw itself forced to subordinate itself to the SA on 21 June. The German National Fighting Units [die Deutschnationalen Kampfstaffen], a paramilitary organization of the party, was now outlawed using, of all things, the Reichstag Fire Decree [Reichstagsbrandverordnung], which had been created to fight the alleged Communist threat. Minister of Economics Hugenberg gave in to strong pressure and resigned at the end of June. In the end, the DNVP, which in March had tried to adapt itself to the new style by renaming itself "German National Front," disbanded at the end of May.

On 14 June 1933 the government put the final touches on one-party government with the Law against Reformation of Parties, which declared the NSDAP to be the sole permissible political party and threatened imprisonment for those who founded new parties or tried to maintain old ones. The smaller middle-class parties and the center had disbanded in the days before.

During the neutralization and elimination measures of these months an estimated one hundred thousand people had been taken into "preventative custody" by the police or illegally arrested by the SA or SS. Since the middle of March 1933, the Nazis had been building special concentration camps for the large number of people who had been arrested.

These measures had been implemented by a remarkable interplay of coup d'état–like, pseudo-legal measures enacted by the government and pseudo-revolutionary actions taken by Nazi grass-roots organizations. The Nazi leadership determined what goals should be pursued, and the SA and SS harassed and terrorized the relevant groups or institutions until the state, which was totally in the hands of the Nazis, made laws or decrees to secure order.

As described above, the National Socialists took on their opponents and competitors separately. They would quickly focus their energy on their target while the other groups were allowed the illusion that they were to be spared. Thus after the passage of the Reichstag Fire Decree the Social Democrats placed great value on emphasizing that they had nothing to do with Communist intrigues. When the Nazi attacks took aim at them, it was the unions that tried to maintain a frightened distance.

In retrospect one must conclude that the potential for resistance on the part of Nazi opponents was not great in the first half of 1933. There was no unified front of democratic forces, nor was there a resistance front of labor parties. The Communist Party was focused on its archenemy, the SPD, and saw the nomination of Hitler as an opportunity to once again "demask" the SPD leadership because of its half-hearted policies. By contrast, while the SPD steered a course of strict legality and was waiting with countermeasures for the government to ostentatiously violate the constitution, its organization was steadily weakened by the skillful tactics of the Nazi leadership until it could no longer act. In any case, the classic response of the labor movement, the general strike, had become a rather dull instrument at a time when there were seven million unemployed. Resistance at this point could only mean symbolic gestures. By this I do not want to overemphasize the defenselessness of the labor parties; rather it seems more important to me to cast a glance at the causes of these parties' paralysis and demoralization in the prior years.

In addition to the paralysis of the their opponents, the National Socialists' success was largely determined by the fact that their activities were tolerated and even promoted by a large proportion of the leadership elites. Hitler's conservative partners in the government tolerated all the measures I have described. Without the active support or the silent tolerance of the Reichswehr, the police, the justice system, higher civil servants, the diplomatic corps, leading representatives of industry, and large estate owners, the takeover would not have been possible.

The alliance of the Nazis and the leadership elites was based on a division of power: The Nazis monopolized domestic political power, and the groups named above tolerated this and withdrew to secure positions, which the Nazis basically left intact. In the ensuing years there was no land reform, no socialization of industry, no revolutionizing of diplomacy, no mass firings among the conservative elements of the justice establishment or the civil service. The Nazis only later succeeded in penetrating these bastions, and then only when the entire system was changed to prepare for and to conduct the war. But even by the end of the war none of these areas had been totally altered.

4. HOW DID HITLER BECOME REICH CHANCELLOR?

Now we want to examine the causes that led to Hitler becoming chancellor.

This appointment was also not an inevitable step. In the Reichstag elections of 1932, Hitler's party had only been able to win about one-third of all votes. It was not in a position to find coalition partners. The president of the Reich had repeatedly resisted Hitler's ultimatums to give him the chancellorship. The leadership of the state thus still had enough authority and power to oppose the pressure of the streets that the Nazis brought to bear.

Delivering the top office of the government into the hands of the leader of an antidemocratic mass movement was in no way tantamount to the capitulation of the democratic state. The capitulation had long since occurred. The appointment of Hitler was the conclusion of a multiyear process in which a functioning democracy was step-by-step transformed into an authoritarian dictatorship.

In this process of turning away from parliamentary democracy four stages can be discerned: the end of the Grand Coalition in 1930; the subsequent formation of Brüning's presidential cabinet; the replacement of Brüning by von Papen's presidential dictatorship; and finally von Schleicher's experiment.

First we will have a look at the end of the Grand Coalition under the Social Democrat Hermann Müller in the spring of 1930. The coalition, which had been formed by the Social Democrats and representatives of the middle-class parties in 1928, appeared to have failed because of the question of how to finance unemployment insurance in the face of rising unemployment. The SPD withdrew from the government after it failed to realize its demand to increase insurance contributions in the face of opposition by the rightist-liberal German People's Party, which saw itself as the advocate of industrial interests in the Müller government.

This dispute about financing unemployment insurance had fundamental importance. The breakup of the grand coalition meant the end of a compromise in social and domestic policy that had been worked out between labor and middle-class interests at the end of World War I and that was constitutive for the Weimar Republic. To comprehend the significance of this process one must return to the beginnings of the Republic.[6]

In 1918 and 1919 the political and economic elites of the Reich had seen themselves compelled to make substantial concessions to social democracy. Introducing the parliamentary system at that time had meant opening the government to Social Democratic leadership, and the elites had made substantive concessions in social policy. Both concessions had been granted in order to check the revolutionary movement but also because the SPD was needed to manage the consequences of the war, i.e., for passing the Versailles Treaty. Paying war reparations had been made a precondition for Germany to again participate in world markets; it was also a precondition for establishing the international creditworthiness of the German economy.

This integration of the Social Democratic labor force into the political and social system of the Weimar Republic was a compromise upon which the foundations of the Weimar Republic rested. It was the result of a domestic balance of power and of foreign policy dependencies that arose in the immediate postwar situation.

In 1930, however, the entire system was decisively changed. The passage of the Young Plan permitted long-term settlement of the reparation question, and the beginnings of high unemployment considerably weakened the position of organized labor. Thus from the perspective of labor's opponents there was no longer a reason to maintain the concessions that had been reached in 1918. Since the relatively strong position of white-collar employees was secured by a high degree of government intervention into wage and social policy, the most important guarantors of this policy, the SPD, had to be permanently robbed of their position in the government. This was tantamount to revoking the parliamentary system, because in the prevailing balance of power no majority was possible without the Social Democrats.

With the presidential Emergency Law [Notverordnungsgesetz] of Article 48, the Weimar constitution offered the possibility of ruling in emergencies even without a parliamentary majority. The second stage in the authoritarian transformation of the Weimar Republic emerged when the leader of the center, Heinrich Brüning, became chancellor and took advantage of Article 48.

But Hindenburg not only handed the Emergency Law over to Brüning; he also gave him the additional guaranty that he would use his right to dissolve the parliament if the emergency decrees were rejected by that body. Right after his inauguration in June 1930, Brüning used this instrument to force through two tax laws the parliament had rejected. But Brüning's decision to dissolve the Reichstag was a fateful one. It meant he was willing to put up with the NSDAP, which had shown sensational successes in the previous state elections, where the party increased its percentage of the popular vote from 2.6 percent to 18.3 percent and, in the Reichstag elections of September 1930, the number of their parliamentary mandates from twelve to 107. This splinter party that had attracted so little public notice had thus in the briefest of periods become a mass movement. These successes of the NSDAP took place at the cost of liberal and conservative parties.

Brüning had made a priority of using the crisis to demonstrate to the world the insolvency of the Reich in order to bring an end to reparation payments and thus to break away from the system that had been created in Versailles. This is an important reason why he neglected to produce an effective policy to contain the crisis. The continuing misery and subsequent radicalization of the large parts of the population that resulted from the burgeoning crisis drove scores of people into the arms of the NSDAP. Since the NSDAP continued to play a role in Brüning's political arithmetic—I cannot discuss the details here—he was not able to decide to effectively resist the National Socialists. A decisive factor for the functionality of the Brüning system was the fact that the Social Democrats had regularly failed to vote against the emergency decrees in parliament in order to avoid permanent dissolution of parliament.

The third stage in the process of turning away from Weimar democracy was the switch from Brüning to von Papen in the early summer of 1932, which meant a change from presidential *cabinet* to presidential *dictatorship*.

The intrigues around President Hindenburg only played a marginal role in this shift. The real reason was the decision by the camarilla around Hindenburg to replace Brüning, who was still dependent on the Social Democrats, with a cabinet that was completely separate from the parliament.

Again, the reason for this shift was the ever-changing foreign policy situation: the de facto end of reparations and the end of the demilitarization provisions of the Versailles Treaty. The inevitable rearmament and the anticipated revision of the Versailles Treaty system could, according to the powers around Hindenburg, only be managed by a government that had broken with all forms of dependency upon the Social Democrats. The fact that von Hindenburg's reelection in April 1932 had only been possible with Social

Democratic votes was viewed as an embarrassment and ironically strength-
ened the desire to eliminate SPD influence. Furthermore, the prohibition of
the SA that had been promulgated by Brüning in the face of expanding
National Socialist violence did not please the Reichswehr for reasons of
"military policy," for the army viewed this Nazi paramilitary organization
as a reservoir for the future supply of personnel.

Forming the so-called Cabinet of Barons under von Papen meant the final
step in the transition toward presidential dictatorship. Von Papen was not
supported by any of the parties in parliament, and he consciously forswore
parliamentary support. In appointing the influential Reichswehr general von
Schleicher minister of defense, he demonstrated support for the Reichswehr.
With his ideas of the "new state," von Papen openly supported turning to an
authoritarian constitutional model.

In accordance with a deal von Schleicher had negotiated with the National
Socialists, von Papen first dissolved the parliament and then revoked the prohibition of the SA so that the NSDAP could enter the election campaign in
full strength. A few days before the elections, on 20 July 1932, von Papen
conducted a coup d'état against the Prussian state government and in this
way removed the last serious republican bastion against the dictatorial forces,
thus creating the power base that Göring so brutally exploited in 1933.

In the elections in July 1932, the NSDAP was able to increase the number
of the votes it received to over 37 percent and its parliamentary mandates
from 230 to 608. It had thus become the dominant political power but was
still far removed from being on its way to assuming power via the polling
booth.

This development also made it obvious that von Papen's model of presidential dictatorship had no future. As long as von Papen could not secure
Hindenburg's agreement to conclusively break the democratic constitution,
his only chance of survival was to repeatedly dissolve parliament and call
new elections, which he did again in September of 1932. In the resulting
elections of November 1932, the National Socialists for the first time showed
substantial losses, declining from 37.3 percent to 33.1 percent.

In the face of this decline in votes, deep dissatisfaction and depression
spread through the NSDAP. The election result showed that despite all the
past successes it would not be possible to accede to power without outside
support. This event also taught von Papen that his plans to permanently
eliminate parliament and to rule via a military declaration of emergency
were illusory—which cost him the confidence of the Reichswehr.

When von Schleicher took over the chancellorship in December of 1932,
the fourth stage in the authoritarian transformation of the Reich had been
completed. Chancellor von Schleicher believed that he could create a
"counterfront" outside parliament and that this organization, encompassing

trade unions, associations, and parts of the NSDAP, would be founded upon the power of the Reichswehr so that it could de facto split the Nazi movement.

We cannot provide a detailed description of the fine points of the plan and its failure. But it is important that von Schleicher's negotiations called upon Hitler and von Papen and that the ensuing two-week-long negotiations concluded with an agreement that there would be a Hitler cabinet.

The appointment of Hitler as chancellor was thus not a result of a democracy that had resisted heroically but was overwhelmed—it was the conclusion of a consistent, multistage renunciation of parliamentary government. The conservative elites responsible for this were by no means initially in favor of bringing the National Socialists to power. But their negligence in the economic and political crises of 1930 to 1933 was responsible for the rapid growth of the Nazi mass movement and for Nazi electoral victories in these years. In the end, the NSDAP seemed to the elites to be an easily manageable guarantor that would secure the foundation among the masses for an authoritarian dictatorship. The background of this transformation process is complicated and dependent upon the altered foreign policy situation and the ever-shifting domestic and social policy axes.

5. THE RISE OF THE NAZI MASS MOVEMENT

Finally I would like to come to the third problem that was decisive for the takeover: the rise of the Nazi mass movement. It would be false to believe that the party's rapid growth could be traced back to the leadership elites of the Weimar Republic, even though they must bear a large part of the responsibility for the success of the NSDAP.

Historical research into the elections has produced a number of methodologically solid yet somewhat questionable results about the composition of the Nazi following.[7] First of all, it is important that Protestants were disproportionately represented among the NSDAP voters. Religion still played a large role in determining political attitudes in the Weimar Republic. About 60 percent of the NSDAP voters came from the middle class, who were thus represented here in numbers about twice as large as they were in the population as a whole. Retailers, craftsmen, and farmers dominated this group. About 40 percent of the NSDAP voters were workers.

But in the last analysis, statistical information is only capable of assigning party preference to several relatively large social categories. Workers, for example, made up more than 50 percent of the population, but this category contains highly trained skilled workers as well as farm workers and baker's apprentices. Furthermore, occupation says relatively little in a period of mass unemployment and massive social decline. To clarify this with an example: What predominates in the mind of a trained white-collar bank employee who must make his living as a part-time unskilled worker, his middle-class background or his proletarian existence? A purely quantitative analysis of Nazi voters can give no answer to these questions.

The great voter movements at the end of the Weimar Republic can only be understood if they are viewed in a comprehensive historical context. If one has a closer look at the party landscape of the Weimar Republic one must conclude that there were four large groupings:[8] the working-class parties, political Catholicism, the liberals, and the conservatives. The backgrounds from which these parties emerged can only be associated with a social class in the case of the labor parties. With the center the ties to the Catholic church predominated, while the conservatives relied on the Protestant rural population, and the liberals traditionally relied on craftsmen and trade. The conservative and liberal followings also included non-industrial workers.

All in all it can be shown that during the period of the Weimar Republic the labor milieu and the Catholic camp were relatively resistant to National Socialism. Both milieus were, however, paralyzed: The workers were split, and the Catholic domain was undergoing a process of dissolution, which however, did not clearly favor the National Socialists.

It was especially characteristic for the development of the Weimar Republic that in the twenties there had been a cumulative process of alienation between the liberal and conservative parties and the social milieus from which they arose.

The old middle class, craftsmen, and retailers who traditionally tended toward the liberal and conservative parties under the leadership of middle-class notables had been especially hard hit by the inflation and the economic concentration process of the twenties. The middle class continued to orient itself toward a harmonic conception of a political order based on social and occupational groups and, threatened by increasing proletarianization, expected a guaranty of class privileges from the state.

The non-Catholic rural milieu that traditionally voted conservative and viewed state authority with some suspicion could now, due to rapid development in modern communication, be reached even in the most remote areas and drawn into the political process when it was hit by the full force of the 1927 agricultural crisis. Its reaction was fundamentally one of opposition: the folkish blood-and-soil ideology was absorbed by the disoriented rural population, and the "rural people" [Landvolk] protest movement spread like wildfire. Both offered great opportunities for Nazi agitation.

This alienation process between liberal and conservative parties and "their" milieus was already visible in the "stable years" of the Weimar Republic. While the left-liberal German Democratic Party [Deutsche Demokratische Partei] declined between 1920 and 1928 from 8.3 percent to 4.9 percent and the German People's Party [Deutsche Volkspartei] from 13.9 percent to 8.7 percent, the German Nationals fell from 20.5 percent to 14.2 percent between 1924 and 1928. In contrast, the splinter parties gained votes, including about 15 percent of the vote in 1928. A new kind of middle-class interest association arose that represented limited interests. In this way several small agrarian parties took shape: the Volksrechtspartei [Party for the People's Rights] that represented the interests of people who had lost their savings during the inflationary period, and the Wirtschaftspartei [Economics Party] that mostly represented homeowners.

This splintering of the liberal-conservative electoral potential clearly points to disintegration within the middle class-agrarian milieu. This justifies the thesis that within the Protestant rural population and among the primarily small-town craftsmen and tradesmen, the integration mechanisms and the mediation of political, economic, and social interests that had been formed under the monarchy were no longer functioning. This can be traced back to the deep shock that these classes and groups felt as a result of the world war, of inflation, and of the depression that began in the twenties. The notables or clientele system, upon which local associations, clubs, and parties were built, had suffered irreparable damage.

In this situation the NSDAP presented the members of the splintered liberal and conservative milieus an attractive offer. The effectiveness of the Nazi mass movement rested on the fact that it represented no class- or group-specific interests but offered the utopia of a renewal of the *Volksgemeinschaft* [ethnic community] that affected all groupings and thus was—or at least sold itself as—a "popular party."[9]

In concluding, it should be made clear that what on the political stage manifested itself as "actions" and machinations must be seen before the backdrop of profound and complex social processes that were in part a result of the war and the postwar period but whose causes transcend these periods. The road that ends in the Bloody Week of Köpenick thus also leads back into the social history of earlier decades.

LITERATURE AND NOTES

The following notes cannot fully represent the diverse literature on the Weimar Republic. It is also not possible to document all the facts I have cited. The best I can do is offer a selection of secondary literature and published sources. First I would like to cite various general surveys that have been published in recent years: Eberhard Kolb, *Die Weimarer Republik* (Munich, 1984); Horst Möller, *Weimar. Die unvollendete Demokratie* (Munich, 1985); Hans Mommsen, *Die verspielte Freiheit. Der Weg der Republik von Weimar in den Untergang 1918–1933* (Berlin, 1989); Detlef J. K. Peukert, *Die Weimarer Republik. Krisenjahre der klassischen Moderne* (Frankfurt, 1987); Gerhard Schulz, *Zwischen Demokratie und Diktatur*, 3 vols. (Berlin,

1963, 1987, 1992); G. Schulz, *Aufstieg des Nationalsozialismus. Krise und Revolution in Deutschland* (Frankfurt, 1975); Hagen Schulze, *Weimar. Deutschland 1917–1933* (Berlin, 1982); Heinrich August Winkler, *Arbeiter und Arbeiterbewegung in der Weimarer Republik*, 3 vols. (Berlin and Bonn, 1984, 1985, 1987). I would like to name a few important titles from the diverse and voluminous literature about the failure of the Weimar Republic and the rise of the NSDAP: Karl Dietrich Bracher, *Die Auflösung der Weimarer Republik. Eine Studie zum Problem des Machtverfalls in der Demokratie* (Stuttgart, 1955; 7th ed. Königstein and Düsseldorf, 1984); *Die nationalsozialistische Machtergreifung. Studien zur Errichtung des totalitären Herrschaftssystems in Deutschland 1933/34*, ed. Karl Dietrich Bracher, Wolfgang Sauer, and Gerhard Schulz (Cologne and Opladen, 1960); Martin Broszat, *Die Machtergreifung. Der Aufstieg der NSDAP und die Zerstörung der Weimarer Republik* (Munich, 1984); Dieter Gessner, *Das Ende der Weimarer Republik. Fragen, Methoden und Ergebnisse interdisziplinärer Forschung* (Darmstadt, 1978); Volker Henschel, *Weimars letzte Monate* (Düsseldorf, 1978); Wolfgang Horn, *Der Marsch zur Machtergreifung. Die NSDAP bis 1933* (Königstein, 1980); Gotthard Jasper, *Die gescheiterte Zähmung. Wege zur Machtergreifung Hitlers 1930–1934* (Frankfurt, 1986).

Die deutsche Staatskrise 1930–1933. Handlungsspielräume und Alternativen, ed. Heinrich August Winkler with Elisabeth Müller-Luckner (Munich, 1992); *Deutschlands Weg in die Diktatur*, ed. Martin Broszat, Ulrich Dübber, et al. (Berlin, 1983); *Industrielles System und politische Entwicklung in der Weimarer Republik*, ed. Hans Mommsen, Dietmar Petzina, and Bernd Weißbrod, 2 vols. (Düsseldorf, 1974; 2d ed. Kronberg and Düsseldorf, 1977); *Die nationalsozialistische Machtergreifung*, ed. Wolfgang Michalka (Paderborn, 1984); *Weimar. Selbstpreisgabe einer Demokratie. Eine Bilanz heute*, ed. Karl Dietrich Erdmann and Hagen Schulze (Düsseldorf, 1980); *Die Weimarer Republik, Belagerte Civitas*, ed. Michael Stürmer (Königstein, 1980); "Die Weimarer Republik—Demokratie in der Krise," *Tel Aviver Jahrbuch für deutsche Geschichte* 17 (1988): 1–342; *Die Weimarer Republik 1918–1933. Politik, Wirtschaft, Gesellschaft*, ed. Karl Dietrich Bracher, Manfred Funke, and Hans-Adolf Jacobsen (Bonn, 1987).

Documents on the Weimar Republic can be found in the following sources: *Akten der Reichskanzlei, Weimarer Republik*, ed. Karl-Dietrich Bracher and Hans Booms, 14 vols. (Boppard, 1968–90); *Quellen zur Geschichte des Parlamentarismus und der politischen Parteien*, three series, numerous volumes (Düsseldorf, 1959ff.); *Ursachen und Folgen. Vom deutschen Zusammenbruch 1918 und 1945 bis zur staatlichen Neuordnung Deutschlands in der Gegenwart*, ed. Herbert Michaelis and Ernst Schraepler, vols. 2–8 (Berlin, 1958–63).

I would also like to make reference to two smaller paperback documentations: *Die ungeliebte Republik. Dokumentation zur Innen- und Außenpolitik Weimars 1918–1933*, ed. Wolfgang Michalka and Gottfried Niedhard (Munich, 1980); *Die Erste Republik. Dokumente zur Geschichte des Weimarer Staates*, ed. Peter Longerich (Munich, 1991).

1. The brochures on the Bloody Week of Köpenick that appeared in the GDR (Kurt Werner, Karl Heinz Biernat, *Die Köpenicker Blutwoche. Juni 1933* [Berlin, 1958] and *Die Köpenicker Blutwoche* [Berlin, 1960]) give an incomplete picture. I hope to present soon a short work about the Bloody Week in Köpenick based on documents not available before 1990.
2. Cf. Rainer Eckert's survey "Berichtswesen im Faschismus," *Bulletin des*

Arbeitskreises Faschismus/Zweiter Weltkrieg, nos. 1–4 (1990): 67–116.

3. Saul Friedländer sees National Socialism appearing, after the intervention of the new, now completed epoch, as a "doubly removed past," in "Martin Broszat und die Historisierung des Nationalsozialismus," *Mit dem Pathos der Nüchternheit. Martin Broszat, das Institut für Zeitgeschichte und die Erforschung des Nationalsozialismus*, ed. Klaus-Dietmar Henke and Claudio Natoli (Frankfurt and New York, 1991), 155–70.

4. Cf. the convincing criticism of Hans Mommsen in the afterword of the 1989 reprint of David Schoenbaum's *Die braune Revolution. Eine Sozialgeschichte des Dritten Reiches* (Cologne, 1980), 352ff.

5. Thus Hagen Schulze in "Das Scheitern der Weimarer Republik als Problem der Forschung," *Weimar. Selbstpreisgabe einer Demokratie. Eine Bilanz heute,* ed. Karl Dietrich Erdmann and Hagen Schulze (Düsseldorf, 1980) 23–49.

6. Hans Mommsen makes a strong case for this in "Das Scheitern der Weimarer Republik und der Aufstieg des Nationalsozialismus," *Tel Aviver Jahrbuch für deutsche Geschichte* 17 (1988): 1–17.

7. Summarized in Jürgen W. Falter, *Hitlers Wähler* (Munich, 1991). For a discussion of the methodological problems of this approach, see pp. 61ff. and 441ff.

8. Cf. Rainer M. Lepsius, "Parteiensystem und Sozialstruktur. Zum Problem der Demokratisierung der deutschen Gesellschaft," *Deutsche Parteien vor 1918*, ed. Gerhard A. Ritter (Cologne, 1973), 56–80.

9. Rudy Koshar, "From Stammtisch to Party: Nazi Joiners and the Contradictions of Grass-Roots Fascism in Weimar Germany," *Journal of Modern History* 59 (1987): 1–24.

3

THE BEGINNINGS OF NATIONAL SOCIALISM, 1919–1923

ERNST PIPER

---

1. MUNICH

It almost seems to be an axiom of criminology that for every misdemeanor or felony that can be linked to an individual the evidence leads to Munich. Munich is the bastion of the reactionary movement.

That not only Ludendorff but also a number of known reactionary politicians live here; that nationalist parties of all shades own a number of newspapers and magazines in Munich; that the resident militia, in spite of official orders to maintain political neutrality, are closely associated with certain political trends; that hostility toward Jews is particularly strong among the average Munich citizen; that, finally, the Deutschnationale Volkspartei [German National People's Party] moved its party congress to Munich with a certain demonstrativeness—all this has simply reinforced Munich's image as the reactionary center.[1]

Thus wrote Carl Christian Bry in October 1921.

The great majority of the Munich middle class experienced the revolutionary upheaval after World War I with passive anticipation at first, and then later with abrupt rejection. This was a result of a mixture of a fundamental rejection of the democracy of the Weimar Republic, of political opposition to the Social Democrats, who were seen as responsible for the "shameful peace" of Versailles, of anti-Prussian resentment, and of robust anti-Semitism. Typical for the mood among reactionary circles was the writer and journalist Ludwig Thoma, who in the newspaper *Miesbacher Anzeige* commented on the assassination of Governor Kurt Eisner, the brutal murder of Gustav Landauer, and the attack on the sex scholar Magnus Hirschfeld with the words:

With the execution of Eisner and the corporal punishment accorded to Magnus Spinatfeld we in Munich offered proof that we do not lack temperament. The Berliners will also have to recognize with gratitude that we got rid of Landauer for them.[2]

For him, the Weimar Republic was contemptible "monkey business."[3]

After the bloody suppression of the Rätebewegung [Munich's revolutionary soviet movement] Munich became a focal point for all the reactionary, antidemocratic, militarist, and nationalist elements in Germany. Or, in the words of a National Socialist portrayal of the period: "Bavaria became the hope of all nationalist circles and Munich the asylum for all persecuted freedom fighters."[4] In this morass of occultism, racist lunacy, nationalist hysteria, and mindless aggressiveness, the movement blossomed that would lead Germany, to whose salvation it had dedicated itself, into the worst catastrophe of its history.

But the early National Socialists were hardly perceptible in the throng of groups, circles, and associations. On 17 August 1912 a man who called himself Rudolf Freiherr von Sebottendorf created the pan-German and anti-Semitic Thule Society that was actively involved in the destruction of the Munich Republic. On 5 January 1919 the tool-and-die maker Anton Drexler, who during the war had represented the Volksbund Deutscher Vaterlandspartei, founded the Deutsche Arbeiter-Partei [DAP or German Workers Party].

The main patron of the Thule Society was publisher Julius Friedrich Lehmann, who was also the leader of the Pan-German Party in Munich. Lehmann was the publisher of the *Münchner medizinische Wochenschrift* [*Munich Medical Weekly Magazine*], which he made into one of the most widely distributed German medical weeklies—where there was an unwritten rule that no Jews could be employed in the company.[5] Lehmann's publishing house specialized in medicine, "folkish politics with special emphasis on purely war-oriented publications during the First World War," and "racial hygiene and genetic research," as well as "racial theory" [*Rassenkunde*].[6] A large part of later National Socialist thought was first developed here. For example, Lehmann repeatedly supported forced sterilization of "inferior people."[7] In 1909 the first of countless publications on racial policy was printed by his house; it was called *Deutsche Rassenpolitik und die Erziehung zu nationalem Ehrgefühl* [*German Race Policy and Education toward a Sense of National Honor*], by retired captain Eberhard Meinhold. Lehmann was in close contact with Alfred Ploetz's Deutsche Gesellschaft für Rassenhygiene [German Society for Racial Hygiene], to whose board of directors he belonged and which was located on the same street as his *Munich Medical Weekly*. He was also closely connected to Richard Wagner's son-in-law Houston Stewart Chamberlain, whose writings on racial policy had a great influence on the Nazis. The most important author in the area was, however, Hans F. K. Günther (1891–1968), the very "race-Günther" who published fifteen books with Lehmann. In 1922 he published *Rassenkunde des deutschen Volkes* [*Racial Theory of the German People*], a book that appeared in bigger and bigger printings each year and by 1933 had already achieved its sixteenth printing. Lehmann had commissioned this work with the then unknown young teacher. Both profited handsomely from the book's unexpected success. Günther was the first to systematically summarize the Nazis' ideas in a consistent theory and to provide these ideas with pseudo-scientific form. When the National Socialists entered the Thuringian state parliament in 1930, Günther was rewarded with a professorship at the University of Jena.[8]

In addition to the *Medical Weekly,* Lehmann published a number of other magazines, for example, *The Struggle for Germanity*, the political pamphlets of the Pan-Germans (he was an active member), *Wartburg*, the polemical paper of the away-from-Rome movement, and finally, from 1917 on, *Deutschlands Erneuerung* [*Germany's Renewal*], "one of the very few magazines that was openly National Socialist."[9]

After the First World War these titles were expanded to include *Folk and Race* and the *Magazine for Racial Hygiene*.[10] Lehmann was also an active member of numerous patriotic associations that ranged from the Flottenverein [Naval Fleet Association] to the German Language Association and the Kampfbund für die Grenzmarkdeutschen (an association in support of Germans who lived near the German borders).

It was a forgone conclusion that Lehmann would join the Thule Society. This society, named for the fabled island Thule, was a front organization for the Germanenorden [Germanic Order] that was founded in 1912. This fraternity, which placed great emphasis on occult rites, would accept as members only people who could demonstrate three generations of Aryan ancestry. The group convened in the Four Seasons Hotel, whose owner was also a member. Other members were state parliament librarian Rudolf Buttmann, later Nazi majority leader in the Bavarian parliament, Ernst Pöhner, Karl Fiehler, Alfred Rosenberg, and Dietrich Eckart. All were later prominent Nazis.

The Austrian Adolf Hitler had been in Munich for a short while; he had come to Munich in 1913 trying to escape Austrian military service and had then joined the German army in 1914 and participated in the war for four years. Later he was employed as a spy against revolutionary soldiers. In the summer of 1919 he was trained as an undercover agent. Hitler's operational control was Captain Karl Mayr, the head of the intelligence and reconnaissance department of the Munich Reichswehr command. On 12 September 1912, Mayr issued Hitler the order to attend a meeting of the DAP, which took place in the Sterneckerbräu beer hall. Four days later Hitler again attended a meeting and joined the DAP, which at the time had fewer than a hundred members. He joined the labor committee as its seventh member and was responsible for propaganda. For the next meeting, which took place in the Hofbräukeller beer hall, Hitler placed an ad in the *Völkische Beobachter*, and 111 people attended the meeting.[11] The featured speaker was Erich Kühn, but Hitler also spoke; on this evening he was to hold his first public address.

On 7 January 1920 the Deutschvölkische Schutz und Trutzbund, the most important organization of the folkish movement, organized the first large-scale anti-Semitic rally, for which seven thousand people came to the Münchner Kindl-Keller beer hall. Hitler, one of the attendees, participated in the discussion and noted what great popular support could be mustered for agitation against the Jews. A little later Hitler organized his first mass rally. On 24 February 1920 Hitler announced the new twenty-five-point plan of the DAP to two thousand listeners in the festival hall of the Hofbräuhaus.[12] The plan took aim at the parliamentary system, immigration, high interest rates, war profiteering, freedom of the press, department stores, and Roman law. Point four said:

> Only those people can be citizens who are members of the same nationality. But only those of German blood can be members of the German nationality, regardless of religious belief. Thus no Jews can ever be of German nationality.[13]

Of all the program points, this was the one with the most grievous consequences. The constitution of the Federal Republic is still determined by this *ius sanguinus* such that in Germany there are over four hundred thousand cases of the juristic monstrosity "foreigner born in the Federal Republic."

2. THE VERY OLD WARRIORS

After the party program was passed, Hitler devised a new public face for the party. It was a very skilled conglomerate patched together from a great variety of existing symbols that ranged from Roman standards to the swastika, which was widespread among rightist groups. Hitler consciously copied Communist propaganda with luminous red posters and black lettering. The flag, too, became red like the Communist flag, with a black-and-white center field organized such that the colors of the old imperial flag were used. The name of the party then became NSDAP (Nationalsozialistische deutsche Arbeiterpartei [National Socialist German Workers Party]). Hitler also increasingly appeared as a public speaker since he was able to draw many people into his spell with his platitudinous and fanatical tirades. In the beginning of March his name appeared on a poster for the first time. Shortly thereafter he clearly recognized his mission: "We are small, but once a man emerged in Galilee, and today his teachings dominate the entire world. I cannot imagine Christ any other way than blond and with blue eyes. But I can only imagine the devil with a distorted Jewish face."[14]

And on 13 August 1920 Hitler made his first direct plea to kill the "parasitic people," the Jews.[15]

Anti-Semitism, which twenty years before the annihilation of the Jews was, so to speak, still in a state of innocence, was extraordinarily popular, especially among students. The University of Munich was a bastion of reaction. When Max Weber criticized the pardoning of Eisner's murderer, Count Arco, his lecture was broken up. A planned lecture by Alfred Einstein had to be called off in 1920 because of "anti-Jewish demonstrations." In 1925 Nobel Prize laureate Richard Willstätter resigned his professorship with an admonition about "animal-like" anti-Semitism on the part of "ignorant, intolerant, and anticonstitutional students."[16] More and more student fraternities excluded Jews. On 5 December 1919 Maximilian Späth, who had served in the First World War as a volunteer and had won high military awards, was expelled from the student fraternity of which he was an officer because of his non-Aryan ancestry. This insult hit him so hard that he went into an adjacent room in the fraternity meeting place and shot himself.[17] This incident caused a furor.

Despite that, a majority of city councilmen were, for financial reasons, not able to resolve to have Nazi graffiti, already widespread by then, removed from public buildings.

Five days after the tragic suicide, the DAP called a meeting in the beer hall called Deutsches Reich. Adolf Hitler was the speaker. This was his second public appearance. His lecture ended with the words: "I stand for the principle: Germany for the Germans!"[18] The main enemy was, in addition to the Allies, the Jews, who "make all the business deals and are agitating for a fraternal war."[19] In reality it was the Nazis who were agitating for such a war, especially in their attacks on their non-Jewish fellow citizens. The synagogue on Herzog Rudolf Street was vandalized. Bands of thugs broke up events of the Jewish Culture Association and destroyed kosher restaurants. Jewish citizens were frequently attacked in broad daylight. There was a particularly grievous case on 14 September 1921 at a meeting of the Bayernbund [Bavarian Association], which

> was violently broken up by the National Socialists who, as usual, employed their storm troopers. The organizers were beaten bloody and thrown down from the podium. Representatives of the middle-class press who were present at that tumultuous meeting emphasized at the ensuing trial that breaking up the meeting had been planned in advance. Forced by the evidence, the court, which had treated these gentlemen with kid gloves, ruled that this was a case of disturbing the peace. Hitler, Esser, and Körner

were each sentenced to imprisonment for three months, and Huber to six months.[20]

This already extremely lenient sentence was soon changed to probation. The incident demonstrated that violence was a genuine component of the National Socialist strategy. In the summer of 1922 the police received sixty-two complaints against the National Socialists;[21] the police as a rule made sure that the investigations got bogged down. In January 1922 Hitler had already declared: "The National Socialist movement . . . will in the future ruthlessly and with violence if necessary prevent all events and lectures that could have a deleterious effect on our already ailing fellow Germans."[22] And in November 1922 he got out the word: "Our motto is: If you do not desire to be a German, then I'll smash your skull in" [Und willst du nicht ein Deutscher sein, so schlag' ich dir den Schädel ein].[23]

This concept of violating the democratic consensus by using demonstrative violence unfortunately proved to be extraordinarily effective. It not only quickly made the then small movement known but also put the democratic forces, who still represented the great majority, on the defensive.

Early on the Nazis got a chance to found their own newspaper. The *Münchner Beobachter* had been printed since 1887. In 1900 publisher Franz Eher took it over. After his death in 1918, Eher's widow sold the paper to the Thule Society, which also published a national edition under the name of *Völkischer Beobachter*. In December of 1920, the NSDAP took over the publishing house; Reichsmark Ritter von Epp contributed half of the purchase price from a Reichswehr fund. The *Völkischer Beobachter* resided in the Buchgewerbehaus on Schelling Street, and from November on, Adolf Hitler was listed as its sole owner. In 1923 the paper was transformed into a daily.

The managing editor of the *Völkischer Beobachter* was Max Amann, who had been in Hitler's regiment during the war. Amann (1891–1957), who, like many other nationalists, came from the Thule Society, thus became the head of a publishing house that had to struggle against financial problems for a number of years but later grew to become an important company that not only dominated the entire party press but also gradually took over a number of book publishers. In the course of his business life, Amann became a multimillionaire.

The editor-in-chief of the *Völkischer Beobachter* was at first Dietrich Eckart (1868–1923). From 1918 to 1921 Eckart had single-handedly and at his own expense published the reactionary, anti-Semitic paper *Auf gut Deutsch*. He was an alcoholic and morphine addict. In spite of that, he possessed considerable social connections and was able to pave many a path for Hitler. He also made sure that Hitler took more care about his appearance and that he improved his German, and he frequently lent Hitler his car and even gave him a raincoat. His extremely aggressive anti-Semitism certainly had an influence on Hitler. But the fact that the much older and established Eckart praised Hitler as the future führer must have made an enormous impression upon Hitler. Eckart also played a key role as a fund-raiser.

The Balt Alfred Rosenberg (1893–1946) was at first assistant editor, then, from 1923 on, editor-in-chief of the *Völkischer Beobachter*. He had been living in Munich since 1919, came from the Thule Society, and had been recruited to the NSDAP by Eckart. Rosenberg was a mystical anti-Semite who liked to blather on about Jewish attempts to dominate the world and propagated the subordination of truth and justice to the pragmatic needs of the Germanic race. His book *The Myth of the Twentieth Century* (1930) was widely read, but Rosenberg never was blessed with high party office or recognition.

The third person who influenced Hitler ideologically was Gottfried Feder (1883–1941). He was considered the economic expert of the party. The phrase "breaking the bondage to interest rates" [*Brechung der Zinsknechtschaft*] stems from him. From 1924 to 1936 Feder represented the NSDAP in the Reichstag [Reich parliament]. Hitler made a deal with industrialists following his rise to power; after that there was no more talk about "breaking the bondage to interest rates," and Feder was shoved off into a professorship. Feder was Hitler's first political friendship, for he was the speaker at the first meeting of the DAP that Hitler attended. Back then, Feder had spoken of doing away with capitalism, which in his eyes was a product of international Jewry. At first he had attempted, without success, to promulgate his ideas with the Eisner government; then he joined the Thule Society.

Hermann Esser (1900–81) was a man of quite a different caliber. Hitler had come to know him while with the intelligence office of the Reichswehr, and Esser had the reputation among Nazis as the best public speaker after Hitler. This "demagogue of the worst kind" (Otto Strasser) was indispensable as a propagandist in the early years. Like Hitler, he early on sympathized with the Social Democrats and had come to the DAP via Ernst Röhm.

Ernst Röhm (1887–1934), who had returned from World War I with severe wounds, had at first joined Epp's Freikorps. Röhm, who had good connections to the Erhardt Brigade, soon became a key liaison figure between the paramilitary organizations and the Nazis. After the destruction of the Bavarian Republic, Röhm was chief of staff for the Munich city commandant. He belonged to a group of counterrevolutionaries who were placed in key positions and who, under the cover of the Emergency Enabling Law, built up a well-organized antirepublican surveillance apparatus. Röhm was responsible for purging and reorganizing the security forces. As the "weapons specialist" for the Erhardt Brigade he supplied the local militias with military materiel. Röhm was also responsible for implementing the Versailles Treaty's disarmament provisions. In dissolving three Bavarian arsenals he brought an enormous amount of weaponry under his own control, which earned him the title of "machine-gun king." He also succeeded in setting up a secret ordnance depot by which he prevented weapons from falling into the hands of the Allies; some of these weapons were secretly sold. One of the buyers was Adolf Hitler, accompanied by Hermann Göring.

Hermann Göring (1893–1946), who came from Rosenheim, had been a successful combat pilot in World War I. In 1921 he came to Munich and registered at the university. In October of 1922 he first encountered Hitler at a demonstration at Königsplatz. Hitler soon gave him leadership of the SA storm troopers, which he set out to organize as a military unit. Göring's house in Obermenzing soon became a collection point not only for needy SA storm troopers but also for Hitler and his closest companions.

The SA was the main bearer of the Nazi terror that articulated itself in beer-hall brawls and street battles and all kinds of attacks on people who held differing opinions. In November of 1921, this group of thugs contained about three hundred men who were organized in twenty-one groups spread around the city. SA people were almost all between seventeen and twenty-four years old and came from the lower middle class.[24] Officers of the Erhardt Brigade took over training of the SA. The SA's first leader was Lieutenant Hans-Ulrich Klintzch, under whose leadership the SA received military training and even entered into defending the homeland in the struggle for the Ruhr area. Göring, who in 1923 as Hitler's top supporter took over the SA leadership, maintained the SA's military trim.

The victors in the battle against the Munich Republic had in 1919 used their favorable position to take over key governmental slots, which turned out to be a vital form of assistance for the Nazis in the early years.

Ernst Pöhner, who was slated to be governor of Bavaria after the Hitler putsch, became chief of police. Wilhelm Frick, who in 1933 became the Reich minister of the Interior and in 1946 was sentenced to death in Nuremberg, became Pöhner's right-hand man and leader of the political department [*politische Abteilung*]. Hans Ritter von Seißner, who was slated to become police chief after the Hitler putsch, became chief of the Bavarian state police, and Ernst Röhm was appointed by Colonel Epp to the general staff of the Bavarian Reichswehr Brigade. These people supported antidemocratic efforts of all kinds with all means available to them. Brigade leader Erhardt, who was on police wanted lists in Berlin, traveled to Munich and set up an office for his terror organization on Franz Josef Street. Police Chief Pöhner set him up with several faked passports;[25] therefore he did not have to worry about police while he set up his "Organization Consul" to commit political murders.[26]

A well-known case is that of nineteen-year-old Marie Sandmayr, who wanted to report a weapons arsenal at the castle of her previous employer. The next day the girl was found in the Fortenried Park, strangled, with a sign around her neck that read:

> You tramp, you dishonored your fatherland,
> So you have been murdered by the black hand.[27]

The murderer, Lieutenant Schweighart, received a counterfeit passport at the headquarters and escaped across the border. The following year he returned with a Hungarian passport and fatally shot USDP member of parliament Karl Gareis in front of his apartment in Schwabing.[28] Workers' organizations protested with a three-day general strike, but the police made sure that the investigation got bogged down.

In the first years of the Weimar Republic, right-wing radicals committed 354 murders. In twenty-four of these cases lenient sentences were passed, while in twenty-three cases the admitted murderers were acquitted. In 307 cases no charges were brought. General Epp explained before the Reichstag that he considered these vigilante murders "to be an act of self-defense and a moral right."[29] Ernst Röhm wrote in his memoirs with unsurpassed cynicism:

> Many a good citizen who personally wanted to betray a fellow citizen poured his heart out to the wrong Entente officer and instead of getting paid he received his reward behind bars. There were also some aristocrats who reported weapons to the Entente and who were found beaten to death. "Vigilante murders," people say today—and the average citizen gets the creeps when he hears of such things. Once a concerned do-gooder came to the office of Police President Pöhner and told him in a whisper: "Mr. President, there are political murder organizations!" "Is that so," answered Pöhner, "but I fear there are too few!"[30]

When, two years after the murder of Foreign Minister Walter Rathenau, the police brought federal charges against Organization Consul, sentences between two and eight months were meted out for conspiracy, but these sentences were postponed until the Reich president decreed an amnesty.

3. BEYOND MUNICH

This climate of street terror and general lawlessness was ideal for the antigovernment activities of the Nazis, in which Adolf Hitler's position became more and more dominant.

From February 1920 until the end of that year, the party organized no fewer than forty-six public rallies. Hitler himself spoke more than fifty times in and around Munich. His recipe for success consisted of propaganda tirades that left political opponents no time to think. Hitler's demagogic talents far exceeded those of all other speakers of his time. His ability to win over the participants at mass rallies contributed to the development of a führer cult. His inflammatory speeches used all the usual formulas and always explicitly placed blame on his opponents: the "November criminals," "world Jewry," etc. This mass agitation brought many members to the party. Where in the beginning a back room was big enough to accommodate meetings, the number of members had increased to two thousand by 1920, and three years later it was over fifty thousand.

On 18 April 1920 the first local chapter [Ortsgruppe] of the NSDAP outside Munich was founded in Rosenheim. Between 2 May and 31 August, Hitler spoke no fewer than six times in Rosenheim. In September the local chapter already had two hundred members.[31] Soon an SA group was also set up; in the following years it was often ordered to Munich to participate in beer-hall brawls. Only five days after his first appearance in Rosenheim, Hitler was invited to speak to the Deutschvölkischer Schutz- und Trutzbund in Stuttgart, where soon a local chapter of the NSDAP was also founded.[32] In the same year Hermann Esser also founded the local chapter in Kolbermoor. A gigantic meeting-hall brawl that the Nazis staged in Göppingen in 1922 gave impetus to the founding of a local chapter in Tübingen.[33] The managing director of the National Association of German Officers, Dietrich von Jagow, who came from the Erhardt Brigade, led a large part of the Wurttemberg right-wing camp to the NSDAP.[34] He also built up the party, which, after being prohibited in Tübingen in April 1923, called itself "Hiking Club Schönbuch" [Wanderverein Schönbuch].

In the years following the First World War there was a plethora of rightwing radical parties and circles. An important organization was the Deutschsozialistische Partei [German Socialist Party, or DSP], which had been founded by Freiherr von Sebottendorf. Their program was published in December 1918 in the bulletin of the Germanic Order.[35] Quite unlike Drexler's DAP, the DSP from the beginning claimed to be represented in all of Germany. Their first party congress in 1920 was attended by representatives from Bielefeld, Duisburg, Kiel, Leipzig, and Wanne-Eickel. The most important local chapters, however, were in Munich and Nuremberg. The latter was led by Julius Streicher, who also published the newspaper *Der Deutschsozialist* [*The Germanic Socialist*]. Streicher already had a long road behind him that had begun with the democrats. On 20 October 1922 he and his supporters founded the Nuremberg local chapter of the NSDAP. Half a year later the first issue of his *Der Stürmer* appeared, a paper that even for Nazi circumstances was an unusually primitive and revolting rag. But it was also a paper that suited the sexual pathology of Streicher. Since *Der Stürmer* belonged to him personally, Streicher quickly became a millionaire.

Hitler traveled tirelessly to gain supporters for his ideas. By 8 November 1923 he had given 188 speeches at party meetings and rallies, 132 of them in Munich, forty-one in Bavaria, eleven in Austria, three in Stuttgart, and one in Elberfeld. The towns he most often visited outside of Munich were Rosenheim, Landshut, Nuremberg, and Vienna.[36] In the north German area the NSDAP was hardly present and thus dependent upon electoral coalitions, for example, with the Deutschvölkische Freiheitsbewegung [German Folkish Freedom Movement].[37] The Deutsche nationalsozialistische Arbeiterpartei [German National Socialist Workers Party] in Austria was a big problem for Hitler because when Hitler arrived on the scene it could look back at a long history. The parties met in Salzburg at an "international conference for representatives of the National Socialist Parties of Greater Germany" on 8 August 1920 and swore unity, but in reality Hitler had quite different ideas for securing his own position of power.[38] He needed the Austrian Nazis just as little as he needed the folkish parties with which many of his party friends wanted to cooperate. Both groups would have just diluted Hitler's influence. At the height of these disputes, Hitler resigned his membership in the NSDAP and made a precondition of his rejoining that he be given "the position of first chairman with dictatorial powers," which the now leaderless party granted him *nolens volens*.[39] Drexler became the honorary chairman and Hitler the chairman, whose exclusive responsibility and power was firmly anchored in the newly revised statute. Hitler's ultimatum also set as a condition that "Munich should always be the seat of the movement" and that any and all attempts to change the name or the program of the party were to be prohibited.[40]

4. THE FÜHRER AND HIS FOLLOWERS

Hitler clearly emerged as the victor from the sectarian battles. At that time Hitler's closest confidantes, particularly Esser, Eckart, and Heß, began to systematically propagate the myth that fate had chosen Hitler to lead his nation—a notion that later culminated in the führer cult. At the same time, the party was reorganized. The headquarters, with Max Amann and Philipp Bouhler as directors, was expanded, while regular bulletins and propaganda directives appeared. Hermann Esser was named director of propaganda.[41] In December 1921 Hitler traveled to Berlin. This was the first of several appearances at the National Club 1919. This club unified the antidemocratic establishment: generals, high civil servants, and junkers. Hitler negotiated with leading representatives of the patriotic associations, to whom he explained his "solution of the Marxist and Jewish problem." A participant later reported: "Back then he detailed all the things he was to make reality in 1933, including the concentration camps, whose necessity he particularly emphasized to facilitate the easy accession to power."[42]

His propagandistic successes—once Hitler addressed sixty thousand people— manifested themselves in increasing donations from industry. Not only publisher

Bruckmann and piano producer Bechstein, old admirers of Hitler, but also the locomotive producer Borsig and others, especially Fritz Thyssen, donated money. In October 1923 Thyssen came to Munich, where he met with Hitler for the first time, to inform himself about the planned putsch, for which he contributed one hundred thousand gold marks.[43]

By grabbing power in the NSDAP in 1921 Hitler prevented the party from being absorbed in the broad movement of patriotic organizations and himself from being degraded to being a drummer for reactionary-traditionalist forces. As a result, these forces split up into the Unified Patriotic Associations of Bavaria [Vereinigte Vaterländlische Verbände Bayerns], which included in its seven subgroups a large number of pan-German, loyalist, and other organizations, plus academic, officers', youth, and economic associations in addition to the cooperative of patriotic veterans' associations. This cooperative distinguished itself from the competition by more than its stringent anti-Semitism. It was also soon dominated by the Nazis. The "activist core" of the cooperative, in which the old Munich resident militia had been absorbed, was formed by the SA, the "Reichsflagge," whose deputy chairman was Röhm, and the Bund Oberland.[44] The managing director of the cooperative was Christian Roth, who had been justice minister under Kahr and who joined the NSDAP in 1924. Its military leader was Hermann Kriebel, previous chief of staff of the residents' militias and a close confidante of Ludendorff's. Bringing the SA into this cooperative promoted its transformation into a paramilitary organization. It now broke with the Erhardt Brigade and received, under Göring's leadership, a military command structure. Finally the groups that were determined to wage active, armed battle against the "November Criminals"—SA, Bund Oberland, and Reichsflagge—broke with the cooperative and formed the Deutscher Kampfbund [German Combat Federation]. Ludendorff was behind this new foundation at the German Conference on 1 and 2 September 1923 in Nuremberg. By this time, Ludendorff had placed himself squarely on Hitler's side. Neither of these men made a secret of their desire for a coup d'état. After 26 September, political leadership was clearly in Hitler's hands.

The SA had had its first big appearance outside Munich the year before at the German Conference in Coburg, where eight hundred SA men destroyed everything in the way of the march into town. "A quarter of an hour later, there was nothing red left to see on the streets," reported a proud party history.[45] By this time, the NSDAP had already been prohibited in Baden and Thuringia. Between November 1922 and April 1923, the party was also prohibited in Prussia, Saxony, Mecklenburg, Hamburg, Bremen, and Hessen. The party filed suits against these and other prohibitions, but the suits were all rejected by a federal court. The court ruled with remarkable vision that the activities of the NSDAP were not in conformity with the law, that this party was prepared to pursue its goals with violence, and that hatred of the Jews was a central part of its platform. The end of the verdict read: "The party is obviously and clearly working toward a nationalist dictatorship."[46] Of course everybody in Bavaria knew that, too, but the political leadership there was clandestinely sympathetic with this goal. In the seven weeks before the putsch, the NSDAP gained 4,726 new members. Ten percent of them were Munichers. But among the military men in the party, Munichers made up 38.5 percent, and among the party's higher civil servants 26.3 percent![47]

5. 1923—THE FIRST BIG CHANCE

1923 was the great crisis year of the Weimar Republic, the year in which the Republic's existence was called into question. On 11 January the French had marched in the Ruhr area. Two days later Reich Chancellor Cuno announced "passive resistance," which, in the light of galloping inflation and the catastrophic economic situation, was hopeless. From 27 to 29 January the first Reich Party Conference of the NSDAP was held in Munich. On the evening before its opening, Hitler spoke at all twelve public rallies. Six thousand SA men were prepared to bloodily suppress any deviant opinion. Historian Karl Alexander von Müller, who sympathized with the Nazis, participated in the spectacle:

> Their own battle songs, their own flags, their own symbols, their own salute . . . military-looking monitors, a forest of bright-red flags with a black swastika on a white background, the strangest mixture of soldierly and revolutionary, of nationalist and socialist elements—also among the spectators: largely from the declining middle class, in all its social subclasses—will this class be welded together here? For hours uninterrupted march music, hour-long talks by subordinate leaders—when would he come? Had something intervened? No one can describe the fever that spread in this atmosphere. Suddenly, at the rear entrance, there is commotion, there are commands. The speaker at the podium breaks off his talk in midsentence. Everyone jumps up with calls of "Heil!" And right through the screaming masses, the screaming flags comes the much-anticipated man with his entourage, walking at a brisk gait to the stage, his right hand raised in a stiff salute.[48]

The Party Congress had been authorized after Hitler had given his word of honor that he would not undertake a putsch attempt. The truth of the matter was demonstrated on 1 May, when the SA, using weapons stolen from barracks, attempted to violently break up the socialist May Day celebrations—which, however, failed due to the intercession of the Reichswehr. Twenty thousand SA men had gathered, some even armed with machine guns. Hitler appeared wearing the Iron Cross and a steel helmet. It was generally expected that the putsch would begin now, after Mussolini's march on Rome six months before had heated up the situation. But in the last moment Hitler sounded the retreat.

The summer of 1923 was a time of great social unrest and duress. The "passive resistance" against the French occupation of the Ruhr area brought Germany into ever-greater economic difficulties. Inflation reached astronomical proportions. Many people were suffering from hunger. On 7 September Hitler purchased his first Mercedes-Benz for ninety-three million Reich marks.[49]

On 26 September the new Reich chancellor, Stresemann, announced the end of "passive resistance." On the same day, the Bavarian state government decreed a state of emergency and appointed the previous minister president Kahr General commissar of state. He had become the Bavarian dictator. Kahr outlawed numerous left-wing newspapers, broke off diplomatic relations with the socialist government of Saxony, and rescinded the implementation regulations of the Law to Protect the Government. On the other side, Kahr refused to pay any attention to the prohibition of the *Völkischer Beobachter* that had been decreed by the minister of the Reichswehr when that paper had ruthlessly attacked the Reich chancellor. When the minister of the Reichswehr removed the Bavarian military district commander von Lossow from office for this, he was reappointed by Kahr. Furthermore, Kahr ceremoniously took control of the Bavarian part of the Reichswehr until a final agreement could be reached. At the same time there were intensive contacts between the forces supporting Kahr and Lossow, the north German antidemocratic forces, the radicals Hitler and Ludendorff, and heavy industry, in which Stinnes's confidante Minoux played a significant role. At first the groups desired to achieve a "cold coup d'état" that was to take place after industry and agriculture had used economic pressure to bring the government to its knees. Hitler was only supposed to take the role of propagandist, and Ludendorff was to be excluded entirely.[50] But no final agreement was achieved.

When on 2 November the Social Democrats left the Stresemann cabinet, tensions mounted further. Many expected a military dictatorship under General von Seeckt. In Bavaria units had already gathered on the Thuringian border to march to Berlin. More and more voices demanded that now was the time to strike. Kahr continued to support a Bavarian right-wing dictatorship that would lead to the restoration of the monarchy as well as a dictatorial government in the Reich that followed the Bavarian model, while the Nazis, after the expected fall of the government, wanted to set up their own government. On 6 September Kahr got Hitler to promise to do nothing on his own. The day after that, the leaders of the Deutscher Kampfbund met under Hitler's leadership and decided to stage a putsch. This meeting, which took place in Hermann Kriebel's apartment, was attended by Kriebel, Hitler, and five other men: General Ludendorff; Major Hans Streck, chairman of the Bund Oberland; the veterinarian Dr. Fritz Weber, who belonged to the elitist-reactionary Academic Guild and was married to the daughter of the publisher Lehmann; and Hitler's confidantes Max Erwin von Scheubner-Richter and Hermann Göring. The putsch was set to take place in Munich and be followed by takeovers in all large Bavarian cities. Frick, still chief of the political department of the Munich police commission, was to make sure that the police did not intervene, while Colonel Roßbach was to occupy the infantry school. Martial courts were to be set up to maintain control over the civilian population.

Kahr had scheduled a rally, supported by the patriotic associations and the Bavarian People's Party, for the evening of 8 November in the Bürgerbräukeller beer hall. Almost the entire Bavarian cabinet as well as many leading representatives of Munich public life were present. Kahr had just begun his speech on the political situation when armed Nazis sealed off the hall. Hitler forced his way to the podium and pressured Kahr, Lossow, and Seißer into an adjoining room. Initially the three resisted the putsch plan, and Hitler returned alone to the hall, where he had only a small part of the public on his side:

> A dangerous wave of agitation spread through the room when he returned to the podium. It did not subside when he began to speak. I can still see his movements as he pulled the Browning from his holster and fired a shot at the ceiling. If you do not come to order, he hollered angrily, I will have a machine gun set up in the gallery. What then followed was a masterpiece of public speaking. . . . He began quietly, without pathos. What is happening, he stated, is not aimed at Kahr, who enjoyed his complete confidence and was to become the vice-regent of Bavaria. By the same token, however, a new Bavarian government had to be established: Ludendorff, Lossow, Seißer, and he. I cannot remember ever having experienced such a sudden shift in the mood of those assembled. Granted, there were still many who had yet to be converted. But the mood of the majority had been completely transformed. Hitler had turned it around with a few sentences just like one would turn a glove inside out.[51]

A little later Kahr and the others returned to Hitler's side at the podium. He claimed leadership over national policy for himself. Ludendorff was named as the leader of a "national army," while he declared Lossow to be "military dictator" and Seißer to be Reich minister of police. Kahr was named vice-regent for the Bavarian monarchy, and Pöhner minister president.[52] The current minister president, Knilling, and the other ministers present were arrested.

Kahr, Lossow, and Seißer—released by Hitler's good graces—went to the military barracks of Infantry Regiment 19 and denied their participation in the putsch so that the march to Berlin, which was supposed to begin on the morning of 9 November at the Bürgerbräukeller, never made it past the Feldherrenhalle, where the state police were waiting. Hitler, Ludendorff, Göring, Scheubner-Richter, Kriebel, Weber, Streck, Rosenberg, Feder (who had just been appointed justice minister), and Heinrich Himmler (who in 1929 would be named Reichsführer of the SS and became the minister of police after Hitler's power grab), all marched in front of the motley crowd that was made up of several thousand men from paramilitary associations and a very few Reichswehr officers. Julius Streicher, who had arrived from Nuremberg and that morning had held one of his infamous anti-Semitic tirades at Marienplatz, was there too. No other Nazi leaders took part in the march to the Feldherrenhalle. Röhm held the military district command occupied with four hundred men from the Reichsflagge. Heß was guarding the arrested cabinet in publisher Lehmann's villa.

At the shootout at the Feldherrenhalle, three policemen and sixteen putschists lost their lives. Among them was Theodor von der Pfordten, a judge at the Bavarian state supreme court. In his pocket was found a draft for a new constitution that was very close to the one that became German law after 1933.[53]

There was also a rumor that Hitler himself had been wounded. In fact his own people, who had tried to pull him from the line of fire, had sprained his arm. Hitler fled to the villa of Ernst Hanfstaengl in Uffing on Lake Staffel, where he hid in a closet but where he was nonetheless arrested. Ludendorff and others experienced the same fate. Several putschists fled abroad, especially to Austria. Outside of Munich the situation remained calm with the exception of a revolt in Regensburg. This was because the SA and the Bund Oberland only possessed limited forces, so that they had to concentrate all the units at their disposal in Munich.

Despite the pitiful failure of the putsch, which later seemed even to Hitler to be a farce, Hitler remained a hero for many. The leaders of the patriotic wing who had at first allied themselves with Hitler and then broken with him were seen as traitors. (The Nazis never forgave Kahr this "act of treachery" and murdered him in 1934 during the so-called Röhm putsch.)

Everywhere on the streets one could hear cries, "Down with Kahr, up with Hitler." There were frequent violent clashes with the police and mass demonstrations by disappointed people. Now more than ever the supporters of the Nazi movement swore loyalty to their "führer."[54] Hitler himself remarked later: "It was a great stroke of luck for us National Socialists that this putsch failed."[55] The reasons that he gives are good ones: (1) Cooperation with Ludendorff would have been impossible in the long run; (2) the NSDAP was still much too weak to take over the power in all of Germany; (3) these "events . . . with their blood sacrifice" were "the most effective propaganda."[56]

6. TRIAL AND NEW BEGINNING

The trial of the putschists took place in the People's Court in Munich, not in the Court for the Protection of the State in Leipzig, which should have had jurisdiction, since the Bavarian state government simply ignored the arrest warrant that had been issued against Hitler. The trial greatly increased enthusiasm for Hitler. Typical for this is a song that Weiß Ferdl performed night after night to thunderous applause:

> German men today stand
> Before the witness stand
> Where they bravely confess their deeds,
> For there is nothing to deny!
> What did they do wrong?
> Or is it a crime
> To want to save the German fatherland
> From shame and misery?

> [Deutsche Männer stehen heute
> vor den Schranken des Gerichts,
> mutig sie die Tat bekennen,
> zu verschweigen gibt's da nichts!
> Sagt, was haben sie verbrochen?
> Soll es sein gar eine Schand,
> wenn aus Schmach und Not will retten
> man sein deutsches Vaterland?][57]

The *Münchner neueste Nachrichten* newspaper wrote: "We will not try to hide the fact that our human sympathies lie on the side of the accused in this trial and not on the side of the November Criminals of 1918."[58] In this atmosphere it was almost impossible to conduct a tightly organized trial that would bring out the gravity of the crimes on trial. And that was most likely not the intention of chief judge Georg Neithardt in any case. Neithardt had been appointed chairman of the People's Court after the suppression of the Munich Republic and was responsible for the scandalous verdict in favor of Eisner's murderer Arco. During the Hitler putsch trial not only emissaries of the justice ministry but also the attorneys of the accused had free access to the judges' chambers.[59] This impression is further supported by the fact that after 1933 Neithardt was shown favor in a promotion. On 1 April 1924 the verdict against Hitler and his fellow accused was announced; it was a caricature of a decision in a proper trial. Hitler, Weber, Kriebel, and Pöhner were deemed to be the ringleaders and sentenced to five years—not incarceration in prison but to the more honorable *Festungshaft*, a form of arrest reserved for political prisoners. Brückner, Röhm, Pernet, Wagner, and

Frick all received one year and three months of *Festungshaft*, while Ludendorff
was judged to be not guilty and left the courtroom to ovations.

The court chose the low end of the sentencing guidelines to pass these
sentences. In addition it approved probation, "because all of the factors that
speak for the defendants," probation so that Brückner, Röhm, and Frick
could leave the courtroom free men.[60] Finally, the court ignored the Law
for the Protection of the Republic, particularly the provision of the law that
would have demanded that the foreigner Hitler be deported, since "the Law
for the Protection of the Republic, in the view of this court, cannot be
applied to a man who thinks and feels in so German a way as Hitler."[61]

Frick, who during the trial had openly admitted to having provided protection for Hitler, was at least supposed to be removed from state service.
But upon his appeal, a disciplinary court overruled the verdict, arguing that
the "confusion and panicky atmosphere, especially at the police headquarters, should be considered a mitigating factor in favor of the defendant."[62]

After the Hitler putsch the NSDAP was prohibited even in Bavaria. It now
called itself the "National Socialist Freedom Movement." In Munich it was
called the "Folkish Bloc" and in Nuremberg the "Streicher List." Streicher
even had the party chairmanship in his control as long as Hitler was in prison.

Five days after the sentencing of the putschists, on 6 April 1924, elections for the Bavarian parliament took place. They clearly demonstrated
how far the erosion of the foundation of the Weimar democracy had progressed.
The BVP had fallen from sixty-five to forty-six mandates, the SPD from
twenty-six to twenty-three, and the Democrats from thirteen to three. The
only big winner was the National Socialist Freedom Movement, which in
its first electoral attempt received five hundred thousand votes (17.1 percent).
Thus it received twenty-three mandates, the same number as the Social
Democrats. In Munich the Folkish Bloc received 50 percent of the votes!
In the elections for the Reichstag one month later, the now forbidden party
campaigned with the breakaway right wing of the DNVP under the name
of "German Folkish Freedom Party" and won 6.5 percent. The Nazis con-
trolled nine of the thirty-two Reichstag seats the new alliance won. The alliance achieved its peak gains in Franconia: Kulmbach 34.7 percent, Bayreuth
32.9 percent, Ansbach 32.7 percent, and Hof 32.1 percent.[63]

In the meantime Hitler and his fellow warriors had arrived at the fortress
in Landsberg, where there was soon a busy casino business. The day began
with a working breakfast under the swastika. Then visitors were received,
on some days as many as twenty. In the evening gay celebrations were put
on. Count Arco had been forced to give up his well-appointed cell to Hitler.
The prison director had additional cells cleared out for the stacks of mail
and the countless gifts and flowers that arrived from everywhere. But political work was also on the agenda. The entire party prominence paid their

respects to Hitler and received directives from him. Even the Reichswehr took advantage of Hitler and his forbidden organizations to keep weapons hidden from Allied inspectors.[64] A police report of September 1924 remarked that Hitler was "today more than ever the soul of the movement."[65]

September was the end of the six-month period the court had specified before the Nazi leaders could be released on probation. Efforts to achieve his release were initiated. A position paper of the prosecutor's office argued that Hitler, Weber, and Kriebel had "misused the extraordinary freedoms (in particular the freedom to receive visitors) that had been granted them to reorganize the political associations that they had used for their treasonable undertaking on 8 and 9 November 1923."[66] But this knowledge, which was based in part on National Socialist publications, made little difference to the court. The state court, responding to an appeal by the state attorney, and even the state supreme court ruled in favor of early release, and on 20 December 1924 Hitler was a free man again.

He had served just one year of his five-year sentence. The Bavarian justice system treated probation and parole in a very arbitrary way. National declarations of amnesty were often completely ignored, while right-wing radical criminals were often released as soon as possible. The system took on the left wing with extreme brutality. Thus a defendant was sentenced to six years in prison because, as a member of the Würzburg Workers Council, he had for two years acted as the newspaper censor. And what happened to him was not unlike what happened to many of his fellow defendants: probation was rejected.[67]

Now came the golden five-year period of the Weimar Republic, a time when interest in the slogans urging revolt declined. In the Reichstag elections in May 1928, the Nazis only received 2.6 percent of the vote. In Peter Scher and Hermann Sinsheimer's Munich book that appeared that same year, we can read:

> Hitler, too, was (for one can hardly say "is" anymore) a transitory phenomenon. They let him talk, they let him putsch—and out! The city of Munich, which he had wanted to purify of foreigners, gobbled him up and digested him. Now he is merely historical excrement.[68]

That was meant ironically. But Hitler's plans were bloody serious—many of his supporters had no idea how bloody.

NOTES

1. Carl Christian Bry, "Die nationale Bewegung in München. Münchner Bilderbogen vom 12. 10. 1921," in C. Ch. Bry, *Der Hitler-Putsch. Berichte und Kommentare eines Deutschland-Korrespondenten (1922–1924) für das "Argentinische Tag-*

und Wochenblatt," ed. Martin Gregor-Dellin (Nördlingen, 1987), 23.

2. Ludwig Thoma, *Sämtliche Beiträge aus dem "Miesbacher Anzeiger" 1920/21*, ed. Wilhelm Volkert (Munich, 1990), 222.
3. Ibid., 117.
4. Rudolf Schricker, *Rotmord über München* (Berlin, no year), 192.
5. *Fünfzig Jahre J. F. Lehmanns Verlag 1890–1940* (Munich and Berlin, 1940), 43.
6. Ibid., 10.
7. Gary D. Stark, "Der Verleger als Kulturunternehmer: Der J. F. Lehmanns Verlag und Rassenkunde in der Weimarer Republik," *Archiv für Geschichte des Buchwesens* 16 (1976): 309f.
8. About Günther cf. Gary D. Stark, *Entrepreneurs of Ideology: Neoconservative Publishers in Germany 1890–1933* (no location, 1981), 197f.
9. *Fünfzig Jahre . . .* (note 5), 89.
10. Ibid., 87ff. and 108ff; Friedrich Lehmann, "J. F. Lehmann 1864–1935," *Adreßbuch des Deutschen Buchhandels* 98 (1936); Stark (note 7), 307f.
11. Werner Maser, *Die Frühgeschichte der NSDAP. Hitlers Weg bis 1924* (Frankfurt and Bonn, 1965), 170; Hellmuth Auerbach, "Hitlers politische Lehrjahre und die Münchner Gesellschaft 1919–1923," *Vierteljahreshefte für Zeitgeschichte* (1977): 11.
12. *Der Aufstieg der NSDAP in Augenzeugenberichten*, ed. Ernst Deuerlein (Munich, 1974), 108ff.
13. Ibid., 108.
14. Cited in Auerbach (note 11), 29.
15. Ibid., 15f.
16. Arno Seiffert, "In den Kriegen und Krisen des 20. Jahrhunderts," *Ludwig-Maximilians-Universität 1472–1972*, ed. Laetitia Boehm and Johannes Spörl (Berlin, 1972), 351.
17. Hans Günther Richardi, *Hitler und seine Hintermänner* (Munich, 1991), 84ff.
18. Ernst Deuerlein, "Hitlers Eintritt in die Politik und die Reichswehr," *Vierteljahreshefte für Zeitgeschichte* (1959): 211 (Document 10).
19. Ibid.
20. *Münchner Post* (14 March 1922) cited in Ernst Toller, *Justizerlebnisse* (Berlin, 1927), 54.
21. *Der Hitler-Putsch. Bayerische Dokumente zum 8./9. November 1923*, ed. Ernst Deuerlein (Stuttgart, 1962), 706.
22. Cited in Alan Bullock, *Hitler. Eine Studie über Tyrannei* (Düsseldorf, 1961), 69f.
23. Ibid., 85.
24. Peter Longerich, *Die braunen Bataillone. Geschichte der SA* (Munich, 1989), 26.
25. Hermann Wilhelm, *Dichter Denker Fememörder. Rechtsradikalismus und Antisemitismus in München von der Jahrhundertwende bis 1921* (Munich, 1989), 137.
26. Günter Neliba, *Wilhelm Frick. Der Legalist des Unrechtsstaats* (Paderborn, 1992), 26.
27. Cited in Heinrich Hannover and Elisabeth Hannover-Drück, *Politische Justiz 1918–1933* (Hamburg, 1977), 153.
28. As in note 26.
29. As in note 27.

30. Stabschef Röhm, *Memoiren* (Saarbrücken, 1934), 77.
31. *Rosenheim im Dritten Reich. Beiträge zur Stadtgeschichte* (Rosenheim, 1989), 11.
32. Maria Zelzer, *Stuttgart unterm Hakenkreuz* (Stuttgart, 1984), 31f.
33. Benigna Schönhagen, *Tübingen unterm Hakenkreuz* (Tübingen, 1991), 39.
34. Ibid., 40f.
35. Maser (note 11), 227.
36. Cf. Hitler, *Sämtliche Aufzeichnungen 1905–1924*, ed. Eberhard Jäckel (Stuttgart, 1980).
37. Jürgen W. Falter, *Hitlers Wähler* (Munich, 1991), 26f.
38. Hitler (note 36), 181.
39. Cited in Maser (note 11), 269.
40. Ibid.
41. Gerhard Paul, *Aufstand der Bilder. Die NS-Propaganda vor 1933* (Bonn, 1990), 59.
42. Hitler (note 36), 530.
43. Fritz Thyssen, *I Paid Hitler* (London, 1941), 114.
44. Longerich (note 24), 33.
45. Walter M. Espe, *Das Buch der NSDAP* (Berlin, 1934), 101.
46. *Der Hitler-Putsch* (note 21), 711.
47. Michael H. Kater, "Zur Soziographie der frühen NSDAP," *Vierteljahreshefte für Zeitgeschichte* (1971): 140.
48. Karl-Alexander von Müller, *Im Wandel einer Welt. Erinnerungen 1919–1932*, ed. Otto Alexander von Müller (Munich, 1966), 144f.
49. Karl Heinz Roth and Michael Schmid, *Die Daimler-Benz AG 1916–1948. Schlüsseldokumente zur Konzerngeschichte* (Nördlingen, 1987), 118.
50. Bruno Thoss, *Der Ludendorff-Kreis 1919–1923. München als Zentrum der mitteleuropäischen Gegenrevolution zwischen Revolution und Hitler-Putsch* (Munich, 1978), 336ff.
51. Müller (note 49), 164f.
52. Albert Schwarz, "Die Zeit von 1918–1933," *Handbuch der bayerischen Geschichte* 4, no. 1 (Munich, 1979): 479.
53. Benedikt Weyerer, "Der Primus als geistiger Killer," *Münchner Stadtanzeiger* (15 April 1993).
54. Wolfgang Horn, *Der Marsch zur Machtergreifung Die NSDAP bis 1933* (Königstein, 1980), 155ff; Harold Gordon, *Der Hitlerputsch* (Frankfurt, 1971), 369f.
55. Cited in Gordon (note 54), 367.
56. Ibid.
57. Cited in Sabine Sünwoldt, *Weiß Ferdl. Eine weißblaue Karriere* (Munich, 1983), 83.
58. *Münchner neueste Nachrichten* (2 April 1924).
59. Otto Gritschneder, *Bewährungsfrist für den Terroristen Adolf H. Der Hitler-Putsch und die bayerische Justiz* (Munich, 1990), 65f.
60. *Der Hitler-Prozeß. Auszüge aus den Verhandlungsberichten. Mit den Bildern der Angeklagten nach Zeichnungen von Otto von Kursell* (Munich, 1924), 272.
61. Ibid.
62. Neliba (note 26), 39.
63. Falter (note 37), 155.

64. "'Von guter Selbstzucht und Beherrschung.' In der Haft machte Hitler die Feste Landsberg zur Zentrale der Bewegung," *Der Spiegel* (17 April 1989).
65. Cited in Gritschneder (note 59), 102.
66. Ibid.
67. Toller (note 20), 64f.
68. Peter Scher and Hermann Sinsheimer, *München* (Munich, 1928), 1.

4

THE FEDERAL REPUBLIC IN ITS FIRST CRISIS, 1965–1968

OTTO SCHILY

Piper Verlag's expectation in inviting me to present this paper was surely less for me to compete with Bonn's (in)famous amateur historians than to call upon my slowly weathering memory to produce direct observations from a period that in many ways has at least a superficial resemblance to the present.

You are thus reading the subjectively colored statement of a witness of those years—a witness who has not been cautioned to tell the truth, the whole truth, and who, one hopes, will not slide into reminiscing braggadocio.

My theme, the Federal Republic's democracy in crisis between 1965 and 1968, is a topic that appears to tolerate no question marks.

People who forever see the stability of the Federal Republic in danger when the economy is down can point to the first significant recession in the middle of the sixties; it led to the fall of the Ludwig Erhard government and to the formation of a grand coalition.

In the words of Werner Abelshauser, who authored an economic history, the history of the Federal Republic is the history of its economy. The Federal Republic, in Abelshauser's words, resembles "an economy in search of a political *raison d'être*." Economic stability was and is still thought to be a synonym for political stability. And indeed there is little doubt that the governmental institutions in the Federal Republic owe their success to the economic prosperity that, after 1948, developed into a so-called *Wirtschaftswunder* [economic miracle]. It is a consequence of the amalgamation of economics and politics that the Federal Republic in 1967 passed a Stability Law that, via Article 109 of the constitution, gained entry into the economy.

The so-called magical square of the Stability Law lays out the metagoals of state and society: economic growth, price stability, full employment, and a balance in trade. With the Stability Law the Federal Republic broke with Erhard's arch-liberal policies and moved to a Keynesian model based on global governmental regulation, which succeeded in getting a grip on the recession.

On the surface, political structures and mechanisms of the Federal Republic proved to be sufficiently flexible to master the crisis in the middle of the sixties. The change in government, in which for the first time the SPD, the largest opposition party, entered the governing coalition, took place with relatively little friction. This opened up a long-term perspective that made possible the formation of a social-liberal coalition under the leadership of the social democrats.

Democracy proved itself to be stable when its fundamental principle, the shift from minority to majority status, functioned. But the Grand Coalition was not a gain for the inner legitimation of the Federal Republic; the contrary was true, despite the fact that this government made remarkable achievements with a law that secured continuing pay for workers who were ill, with the occupational education law, and with the introduction of the value-added tax.

In the realm of foreign policy, too, the Grand Coalition made strides. The appointment of Willi Brandt as vice-chancellor and foreign minister initiated a preparatory phase that led to later détente. The Hallstein Doctrine, with which the Adenauer government had attempted to establish its claim to represent all Germans and to secure the total isolation of the GDR, was loosened to the extent that it finally had to be abandoned altogether, and the Federal Republic took its first halting steps toward establishing official contacts with the GDR. It is perhaps correct to say that the Grand Coalition was the provisional conclusion of the economic and political reconstruction of a West Germany that had been intended to be a temporary construct. This reconstruction, which also contained signs of restoration, was not linked to any ideas or intellectual-culture impulses.

The physical destruction of central Europe by the Nazi regime, which was able to draw the majority of the German population into its criminal acts, left unforseeable devastation in people's minds and souls. Economic success as a kind of surrogate self-confidence soon proved to be a mere facade, which concealed spiritual emptiness and exhaustion—but it also entailed a powerful act of psychological repression.

Remarkably it was Ludwig Erhard who, in the late phase of his political life, recognized the inner hollowness inherent in a political model that aimed at creating a total economization of society and who tried to counter this with his notion of a "shaped society." This concept, however, remained abstract and without effect. This no doubt has to do with the fact that Erhard, who made a great contribution toward overcoming the bureaucratic-militarized planned economy, was curiously unable to gain insight into the fundamental structure of a labor-based society. The success of this kind of society is based on the principle that the general welfare is increased when the individual works for the benefit of others and not merely for himself. Ludwig Erhard saw this as a kind of escape from individual responsibility and thought that if this kind of development continued we would slide into a social order in which everyone has his hands in everyone else's pocket. The social principle would then be "I'll take care of the others if the others take care of me." The dynamics of modern economies, however, are founded on the principle that people do not work as much for their own interests as for the interests of the others (which Rudolf Steiner called "the chief social law"). The so-called "concerted action" created back then by Karl Schiller is in a sense an expression of this dynamic principle.

The amorphous society that lacked inner consistency beyond its economic goals had fairly quickly overcome its economic problems by the mid-sixties only to fall into a crisis of a quite different kind. It is remarkable that this crisis culminated at a time—1968—when the economic recovery of West Germany was visible for all to see because the number of job offerings had outstripped the number of unemployed.

The crisis-driven events of this period have been passed on to us under the names of "student revolt" and "extraparliamentary opposition"; they represent a deep rupture in the mental history of the Federal Republic of Germany. The myth of the generation of '68, admired, feared, or scorned, lives on today. The extraparliamentary opposition and the student movement reached an unusual vehemence that presented the political actors of the period with considerable excitement and a large dose of unpleasantness.

But these crisis years of 1965 to 1968 also brought a resurgence of right-wing extremist forces. The sporadic election successes of the NPD, which gained entry into several state parliaments, were certainly a warning that the spectrum of the right still possessed a democracy-threatening potential.

Be that as it may, these kinds of political developments led at best a shadowy existence. It is presumably true that the NPD gained sporadic success because the CDU/CSU, working together with the SPD in the Grand Coalition, was no longer able to absorb rightist splinter groups as it had in the past and would again in the future. The NPD was probably also a receptive pool for the resentful petit bourgeoisie, which has traditionally tended toward right-wing extremist parties in bad economic times. There is also the possibility that the echoes of right-wing extremist thought had grown because the state had increasingly acted in a repressive and authoritarian way.

The temporary success of the NPD may also have been aided by the fact that after 1961 increasing numbers of foreign workers had been recruited. Thus the percentage of foreign workers rose from an initial 1.1 percent of employed people in 1961 to 10 percent in 1970.

But the NPD's threat to democracy was marginal at best—even if in retrospect we have to recognize that we perhaps treated this political madness, which today is bearing bloody fruit, with benign neglect.

I am speaking in a series with the title "The Resurgence of Right-Wing Radicalism" and now find myself in an embarrassing situation: The alarming election successes of the NPD in the sixties were an episode. It was a spook that soon disappeared. It did not cause a crisis, even if it did cause concern abroad. The Federal Republic's democratic society remained mostly resistant to rightist extremism. The temporary electoral gains of the NPD were thus perhaps symptoms but not causal agents of a crisis.

With this I could end my lecture, briefly and painlessly. But since we are gathered here, I hope you will allow me to speak of the events that were really experienced as a crisis between 1965 and 1968. The crisis was a confrontation of established political power with the student movement and the extraparliamentary opposition, which I, unlike pamphleteer Wilhelm S. Schlamm, will hardly view as paralleling rightist-radical forces.

The student movement and the extraparliamentary opposition had a long prehistory. They were not simply an oppositional movement against the Grand Coalition, even though the coalition was a causal or reinforcing agent. And of course the SPD's breaking away from its eternal oppositional role was combined with a number of accommodating steps. One of them was passing the Emergency Law [Notstandsverfassung]. The disappointment about this deviation from the pure doctrine was greatest with people who only saw the bourgeois state as an instrument of domination in the hands of the bourgeoisie.

But such simple explanatory models seem to me to be unsuitable to describe the massive transformation in those years. I am also in the embarrassing situation of not being able to offer a thorough and systematic analysis of that period—in particular because I have not yet completed my own verdict on the period.

This is presumably the place where I add for caution's sake that I was not a proponent of or a spokesman for the extraparliamentary opposition or the student movement. At the time I had already completed my studies and was working as a lawyer.

I am a member of a different generation than the people who participated in the APO (extraparliamentary opposition) and the student revolt. True, I took part in a number of demonstrations against the Vietnam War and in the rally to protest the shooting of Benno Ohnsorg. I represented the father of Benno Ohnsorg against the police officer Kurras, I was a friend of Rudi

Dutschke's, I knew a lot of people from the student movement, I represented students accused of breaking the peace, I represented attorney Mahler in his trial for demonstrating in front of the Springer Press, and I was a member of the Republican Club (not to be confused with the Republicans who have unfortunately occupied this good name). At this point many people will be wondering why I omitted mention of the RAF trials, which, however, took place in later years, when the student movement was already defunct. Nonetheless, these, too, are part of the heritage of the APO and the student movement.

My perceptions and feelings about what happened back then can thus not be generalized. I find it extremely difficult to link all the various perspectives in such a way that a vivid, clear image might emerge.

What took place between 1965 and 1968 was primarily, I think, a process of profound disillusionment. In the first decades of the Federal Republic there was something like enthusiasm for liberal democracy, a naive passion for the United States of America, even a longing to assimilate into the American way of life.

The frantic jubilation that greeted John F. Kennedy in Berlin was an expression of this passion. With many people the sympathy for the United States changed to deep disappointment when it turned out that U.S. policy did not live up to its high moral principles. The war in Vietnam and the U.S. intervention in Iran and other places were examples of this.

While official politics ignored this or even tried to sell the war in Indochina as a defense of freedom, the criticism of it articulated itself in a rebellious counterpublic sphere. The tensions that resulted were so strong that one is justified in referring to social disintegration.

A second conflict reinforced this disintegration. It became increasingly apparent that 1945 had brought no radical departure from the governmental and social forces that had plunged Germany into the ruination that was the Third Reich. Globke, a commentator on the Nazi race laws, made it all the way to state secretary in the chancellor's office and became a close confidante of Adenauer's.

The newly elected chancellor, Kurt Georg Kiesinger, had a murky Nazi past. Many Nazi generals were taken over into the Bundeswehr [German military], and many members of the old apparatus of state found refuge in the institutions of the Federal Republic. Especially problematic was the fact that many business magnates were able to maintain their position of power in the Federal Republic. Flick is an example. The fact that many Nazis had again become presentable may also have contributed to the NPD's increased membership.

The third element that influenced the constellations of the opposition that was forming outside of parliament was the rejection of ideological anti-communism, which had lost its credibility.

We could also say these three political fields were something like projection surfaces for a kind of critical thinking that had begun to move away from the practiced consensus.

Deficiencies of legitimation, fearful anticommunism, hypocrisy, and the restoration of old power structures, on the one hand, and moral indignity and rebelliousness coupled with critical thinking, on the other, led to the contours of the dispute in the late sixties. It became clear that the republic lacked the ability to communicate. We can also interpret the student movement and the extraparliamentary opposition as a process that attempted to overcome this weakness in communication.

Suddenly something shocking happened. The people, or to be more precise, a small portion of the people, began to make use of its rights. Public thinking availed itself of public places: the streets, university lecture halls, and finally the courts. And the conflict received a new name. The sleepy complacency of German society was disturbed. The resonance would surely have been much smaller had it not been for a strange mixture of disparate movements. The student movement arose neither overnight nor from some calculated plan. It was recruited through subversive actions, the founding of communes, and the Socialist German Student Association (SDS) but also from the movement against nuclear death and the opponents of the Emergency Law. It is characteristic that the APO and the student movement developed neither an independent political theory nor a practical political concept. The student movement and the APO never got beyond adopting bits and pieces of neo-Marxist and neo-Freudian theories. The student revolt was in a sense a masked ball at which the participants joyfully posed with much Marxist nonsense from the props room of history. That explains the limited scope of this movement. The revolt against restoration in the Federal Republic sought its symbols and ideas on the outside and ended up with grotesque identities borrowed from Lenin and Trotsky, from Stalin to Mao, from Che Guevara all the way to Enver Hoxha.

Nonetheless, the seriousness and intensity with which leftist students set out to develop a theory was admirable and not at all in vain, even if they at first maneuvered themselves into a political dead-end street. But the search for congruent philosophical systems had many and highly disadvantageous side effects because the protagonists were blind to the crimes and mistakes of the socialist nations. This accusation does not apply to everyone; Rudi Dutschke, for example, kept both eyes open.

The movement of '68 was not a revolution in the usual sense. It was, in Arnuf Baring's term, a "revolution of consciousness." The student movement had something playful, something theatrical, about it. Despite all its provocations and "limited violations of the rules," it was fundamentally peaceful and open to discussion. The movement appropriated Marx's sentence that social relationships had to be made to dance, and it made a rock concert out of them.

The fear, indignation, and violent rage with which established social forces reacted were a tremendous overreaction. What emerged were reciprocal, complementary distortions in the perception of the opposite side. The middle-class parties saw revolution at the door while the APO feared dictatorship, which, presumably, would come about via the Emergency Law.

It was no doubt also a generational conflict. Youth, and especially students, were tired of the old conventions and compulsions. So it is correct when Daniel Cohn-Bendit and Reinhard Mohr call the—utopian—riots in Schwabing a precursor of the protest movement of 1967–68.

Viewed from today it is hard to understand what convulsions this movement and the students' desire to throw old conventions overboard caused in society. Long hair and exaggeratedly casual clothing were seen as a provocation. The rejection of sexual taboos was a horror to the middle class. The practice of the freedom of assembly, spontaneous demonstrations, which are normal today, seemed to be a case of open revolt then. Society and state reacted with extreme irritation to the fact that a number of insolent people dared to encounter authority with something less than the accustomed humble devotion.

The new aesthetic, the new life-styles, and the desire for emancipation from the old systems of domination were more than just a change of fashion; they were a radical transformation of values. In the essay "Liberation from Abundance," which was published in the magazine *Kursbuch* in 1969, Herbert Marcuse wrote the following:

> And at the risk of being laughed at, I would like to add that this is an "aesthetic" reality—society as a work of art. That is the greatest utopia, the most radical potential of emancipation. What does that mean in concrete terms? As I said, this is not a matter of private sensitivity and sensibility but rather sensitivity and sensibility, creative imagination, and a faculty for style being productive forces to transform society. As such they could lead to the complete transformation and rebuilding of our cities and to the restoration of free land—to regaining nature once technological violence has disappeared and once the destructive force of capitalist industrialization is broken. It could lead to the creation of inner and outer spaces of silence, to eliminating noise and cultural submissiveness, to being rid of the herd mentality, of filth and ugliness.

The remarkable thing about this Marcuse text is that it is already taking aim at the destruction of nature by modern industrial society. Here we find a precursor of the ecology movement, even though ecology was not a topic for the APO and the student movement. Like many an industrial manager, the spokesmen of the student movement were caught up in the illusion that civilian use of nuclear energy was the solution for humanity's energy problems. And anyone who doubted industrialized agriculture could only count on indulgent smiles from the student revolutionaries.

The student movement and the extraparliamentary opposition loved grand gestures and haughty, highfalutin speech. In Peter Schneider we can read: "The realization of the libido program under the conditions of late capitalism and imperialism thus lies in world revolution." No one can understand that kind of thing today. People then thought they were engaged in the class struggle, a part of the world revolution, warriors against imperialism and capitalism. A sentence like "Whether exemplary actions are transmitted into class struggle will depend on the ability of students to break out of their class and organize the struggle at the grass-roots level" (Peter Schneider) exposed no one to ridicule—on the contrary, sentences like this could count on cheers at a teach-in.

The majority of society reacted to the provocations by the student movement with impatience and incomprehension at best, and often with brutality and naked hatred. This was demonstrated in a crass way at an event I can clearly remember. It was the time when carpet bombings of Vietnam were taking place. At Christmas 1967, students had arranged a demonstration in front of the Gedächtnis [Memorial] Church in Berlin with large-format photographs of napalm-burned children. The irritation of the people who were attending Christmas mass was great. They had their Christmas goose in their bellies, expected an uplifting sermon, and did not want to be disturbed while they comfortably digested their food. But now the following happened: In front of the altar posed a young, poorly shaven man with a well-known demoniac face and an unmistakable voice; he began his address with the words "Dear brothers and sisters." He did not get any farther because the assembly that had been so peaceful was in seconds transformed into a hate-filled, venomous mob. People shouted Rudi Dutschke down with faces distorted by rage, hit him, spit on him. An old man hit him on the forehead with a crutch so hard that blood was flowing down his face. Two other men grabbed him by the arms and led him out through the raging mob.

Indeed, the well-situated majority of the Federal Republic responded with violence to the moral appeals from the student movement. In doing so, it refuted its own claim to be a pluralistic and peaceful society.

It was probably the shocking and unpredictable aspects of the student movement that moved the Federal Republic to reflect on its inherent contradictions. The German feeling of submissiveness toward the state was now countered by a refractoriness that expected the German sense of order to recognize that the freedom of assembly guaranteed in the constitution had a higher priority than traffic laws.

Of course a self-critical examination of what happened in the late sixties should not ignore the fact that one result was the removal of taboos against inner-societal violence. The problematic distinction between violence against people and violence against things is part of this, but so is the rhetorical rehearsal of "revolutionary violence," as was evident in the ambivalently attractive yet dangerous text passage from Ernst Bloch:

> The main thing seems to me to be the question: Is hatred in concrete revolutionary situations a means that can be permitted for a period of time? This hatred that is quickly transformed when it is justified, i.e., caused, such that the murky unsightliness and the criminal aspects that are caused by blindness and pure resentment disappear—this hatred must find a transition to anger. Anger has a quite different character than hatred. There is even the category "divine wrath." And anger, when it has been caused—yes, that is an element that led to the storming and destruction of the Bastille, or to the defeat of Zwing-Uri, to revolt for reasons of human dignity, to the upright posture inherent in the act against Gessler's hat. This was not primarily caused by hatred. The main feeling is anger, which has a different physiological location than hate. Hatred is pale, gloomy, cowardly, smoldering; it has beery vapors about it that can be explosive. Anger is open. It doesn't make us pale; it makes us red. Anger relinquishes all circumspection, unlike the repressed and impoverished Nazi petit bourgeois, who is quite circumspect. Anger is not opportunistic; it can suddenly turn against our own interests and is thus related to higher things. . . . All revolutions are accompanied by anger. Anger doesn't necessarily make us blind. Anger is also active and temporally bounded. Hatred smolders on. When anger erupts there is still time to allow our minds to speak, as they have spoken before—otherwise it would be mere hatred.

Established society, deeply entangled in its hypocrisy, was not able or willing to understand this discussion of violence in a critical and self-critical way. Later, as we know, the discussion merged with a very much more fateful development.

The events during the crisis-driven transformation of the sixties can possibly be explained with the German condition that Hans Magnus Enzensberger described in his "Recommendation for Goodness" as a mixture of "mediocrity and madness." His ironic commentaries on these events should not be ignored, if only because he is one of the outstanding leftist intellectuals, a man who decisively shaped the discussion from 1965 to 1968. It is no coincidence that *Kursbuch*, the magazine he edited, first appeared on 12 June 1966. Twenty-two years later, in 1988, Hans Magnus Enzensberger wrote in his essay "Mediocrity and Madness: A Recommendation for Goodness":

> The Federal Republic is blessed with a singular deficiency. The Germans have exploded their history with their own hands. This was a violent act

of demolition that made their country a product of the new. The talk
about restoration, a popular topos in the fifties, was, as we know today,
based on deception. It is true that the old Nazis did the best they could as
bureaucrats, businessmen, and judges to reshape public life according to
their own notions, but this project of "reconstruction" proved too hopeless,
and the return to the prewar period turned out to be a chimera. When the
scaffolding fell in the sixties, what met the eye was a totally new structure.
It is now, after three or four decades, time to recognize that the critics of
West German society, whether they come from the right or the left, were
plagued by bad luck. Their interpretations not only proved to be ineffectual;
they were wrong. They founded their analyses not on cold-blooded observations but on prejudices and their prognoses not on a good nose for the
future but on an obsession. (Which should not lead us to conclude that
their efforts were in vain. What used to be called social criticism, an
expression that has faded for good reason in the last decades, can be seen
as a self-resulting prophecy [this English phrase is in the original text;
"self-fulfilling prophecy" is no doubt what the author had in mind]. The
sense of the statements from this period would then consist of providing
their own refutation.)

Is there still a bridge from the present to the past of the sixties?

There are several coincidences that in a sense appear to be a repetition of
the constellation of crisis in the second half of the sixties. With the fall of
the Wall, Germany completed its national reconstruction. We are in the middle
of an economic recession that is quite a lot deeper than in the sixties. Right-
wing extremist parties have again gained ground. Right-wing extremist violence, murder, and bodily injury have taken on perilous proportions. Some
signs indicate that the Germans have not yet rid themselves of their propen-
sity to nationalist excess. Politics in Bonn seems to have tacitly agreed on
an informal grand coalition that will perhaps soon become a formal grand
coalition.

All in all, society has remained amorphous. It has not gained in inner
consistency. Everywhere people are lamenting the lack of orientation in society. In a short essay he called "A Small Objection to the Grand German
Euphoria," Jurek Becker noted:

Really existing socialism is on its way out, no doubt about it. We do not
have to lament its loss if we keep the real situation in these countries in
sight and not the fiction that their leaders sold as reality. The West won,
and *that* is the problem. We in the West live in a society without objectives.
If there is such a thing as a program, then only: the bottom line. Theoret-
ically one could continue to increase the bottom line until our world lies
in rubble, and the way things look, just that will happen. But despite all
experience and beyond all intelligence the hope existed that the socialist
countries could take another path. This matter has now been laid to rest.

The population there knows no greater longing than to be able to take over the fundamental Western principles: Transform as many goods as possible into garbage. That *is* the bottom line—that and permitting all thoughts to be expressed (coupled with a growing distaste about thinking). We know the phenomenon that converts observe the rules of their religion in the strictest way. This is probably also true for a converted people. A few days ago I was speaking to a friend about the possibilities of German unification, as all Germans are doing these days. He was for it, I was against it. After a while he angrily demanded that I name him the reasons why the GDR should continue to exist. I started thinking and I'm still thinking. If I can't come up with anything, I'll have to change sides and become a supporter of reunification. And I'd have to be for making eastern Europe western Europe. The only answer I can offer is more useful for a poem than a political discussion: The most important thing about the socialist countries is not something visible; it's a potential. Things there are not as determined as they are here. This uncertainty doesn't have to be a good thing, but it nurtures the only hope we have that people will continue to exist after we are gone. Eastern Europe seems to be a last attempt. If it comes to an end, then we can get all our money from the bank and drink it up.

We should not give up the hope that Jurek Becker articulates. Otherwise we will end up with an emptiness in which real evil will literally take possession of people. The enlightening and emancipatory pathos of the end of the sixties has become stale. Closed systems to explain the world proved to be remote from reality. But history has not ended. It cannot be concluded like a trial. Work on the social sculpture (Josef Beuys) is still ahead of us. We will succeed if we seek to shape the society with the formal principles inherent to it. One of these principles will be making culture a social necessity.

5

RIGHT-WING RADICALISM IN THE UNIFIED GERMANY

THOMAS SCHMID

The facts seem to be clear, the acts appear to speak for themselves: For a while now the number of right-wing radical, chauvinist, xenophobic attacks and acts of violence has been increasing. The taboos are falling one after the other. Since Hoyerswerda in the summer of 1991 and Rostock-Lichtenhagen in the summer of 1992, such acts of violence have dominated newspaper reports and TV news.

This violence, chiefly motivated by xenophobia, seems to follow a cyclical pattern. At times the focus is in eastern Germany (as after the events in Rostock) and at times in the West (after the murders in Mölln and, even more clearly, Solingen). We have long since reached a dangerous form of "normalization": As long as human life is not directly threatened, the daily accounting of attacks is considered to be news of the second and third order that can have a disquieting effect but that, on the other hand, can also act as an invitation. When the practice of violence is such an everyday affair, then, or so it must seem to youthful firebombers, it can't be all that bad to get involved in it yourself. A strange connection: on the one side, a desensitization of the public caused by the number of attacks; on the other side, the creeping activization and motivation of potential violent offenders.

Violence from the right has bulldozed the liberal public sphere. The fact that there were no quick massive counterreactions (after Hoyerswerda, for example) appears to signal a weakness in the civic fabric of Germany. This weakness, however, seemed to have come to an end with the chains of light demonstration at the end of 1992. Finally, one would hope, civic society, conscious of its duties, is asserting itself in word and deed; finally it is becoming clear where the majorities in this country stand. There was reason to assume that there would soon be an end to this rightist apparition. The silent majority of democrats would only have to raise its voice and the rightist mob, which has rightly been called cowardly, would take flight. The months following the chains of light offered hope. In the meantime, however, it has become clear that the chains of light were not enough. The murderous assault in Solingen made it clear that the end of rightist violence is not in sight. Many signs point to a continuation of this "normalization." Some signs speak for the assumption that the violent offenders often act in the knowledge of being the outcast kids of society; but they also believe that they are daring to act out the opinions of the majority. Paradoxically, these people perceive themselves to be an avant-garde that can be sure of support from the majority.

Add to this the success of right-wing radical parties and groups. Since the end of the sixties, since the surprising election successes of the NPD, the parliamentary potential of the right wing has been invoked repeatedly. For a long time there were good reasons to assume that this was only a matter of people who are incapable of learning from the past—and who will soon make their contribution to civilization by quickly emigrating to the grave. The surprising election success of the "Republicans" proved that this was not to be as simple as it seemed. In the meantime the rightist parties and election groupings have demonstrated with great regularity that they were not up to the standards of parliamentary life but were at best good for a few laughs. Furthermore, there were grounds for hope in the fact that German-German unification, on paper one of the loftiest goals of the right, rather than helping actually harmed these groups. The deficiency in their programs was all too obvious. And it also became clear that they, far from being buoyed by the conflict between nationalist goals and possessive chauvinism, were paralyzed by it. So it seemed that national unity, the goal that the right had always proclaimed, had pulled the rug out from under the rightists' feet. The first elections after unification also seemed to support this thesis. While in the West the radical right had to come to grips with a radical loss of votes, it was not even able to gain a toehold in the East. Now this euphoria has also passed. The low point of the right turned out to be a temporary low, and there are reasons to believe that rightists will benefit from the malaise of official politics and establish themselves in parliament.

So there is no doubt: Right-wing radicalism is on the rise. Yet I am still not sure that we will gain much if we try to recognize old forms in this new phenomenon or if we try to reduce what is new to these old forms. On the contrary, I presuppose that the widespread talk about right-wing radicalism (which leads to slogans like "Out with the Nazis!") only intimates a decisiveness and certainty in our knowledge. It is a good bet that the old right wing is still present when Nazi emblems and slogans are reactivated and used. Then we quickly get the sense that in Germany the old monster that leftist propaganda has invoked repeatedly has indeed survived unscathed. Only a thin democratic veneer—or so it might seem—has been placed over the Germans' traditional authoritarianism and chauvinism in the four decades of the "old" Federal Republic—a veneer that only held as long as prosperity kept the country's civility from being put to the test. But a unified Germany would quickly show its true countenance; it would slough off its bothersome democratic cloak and turn out to be what it always was: an unpredictable country that abhors democracy and is still prepared to do horrendous things.

There are no doubt symptoms that make this view plausible. But I consider this view to be extremely negligent, for it suggests a certainty of judgment that simply does not exist. It suggests that with this "new" form of "old" right-wing radicalism we are dealing with an essentially familiar phenomenon that we know from our history. And this leads to necessary, probing questions being smothered by prestabilized queries. I would like to suggest another way of looking at this: a groping search for truth. I presume that right-wing radicalism is neither familiar nor adequately researched and that we are not sufficiently informed about its reasons, its depth, and its extent. Drawing quick parallels to 1933 and the Nazis may well sound exalted and offer a facile recognition value, but it certainly does not shed light on the problem. Without in the least wanting to relativize or exculpate, I assert that none of these commonalities—the things that at first glance link the new with the old Nazis—is important. These differences are far more important—the things that distinguish the new from the old right. I would like to preface the following questions with a thesis: In the current right-wing radicalism we are dealing less with a force from the German past than with something totally new, with a product of postwar modernism.

Using this perspective I would like to address the following questions:

- Is this new right-wing radicalism a specifically German phenomenon? Or is it an all-European problem? If the answer to this question is yes, then why is that so? And can we speak about this without—as has happened many times in the past—diverting attention from the dark German past?
- Is the recent upsurge of right-wing radicalism related to German-German unification? Is the unified Germany merely once again making clear what has survived underground: the right-wing stream of eternally German continuity? Is the new right-wing radicalism an expression of a new German strength or a new German weakness that has arisen from unification?
- Does right-wing radicalism have the strongest forces at its disposal in the East or in the West? Where is it strongest and most resolute? Have forty years of democratic experience made the West more civil? Or was it all only whitewash? What kind of havoc did socialism cause in the East?

- And finally: Is the "new old" right-wing radicalism a classical (and political) right-wing radical movement? Does this right-wing radicalism come from the margins of society or from its center? Has it drawn its sustenance from or been held in check by the conservative parties? Is this development a signal that the appeal of the great popular parties is in decline? Are only the social losers susceptible? What about the well-to-do, the successful, the yuppies? Thus back again to the question: Is this perhaps a modern phenomenon that we scarcely recognize because it has appeared in an antiquated costume?

1. THE GERMAN RIGHT AFTER 1945

First, a few remarks about the right and the extreme right in Germany after 1945. Has the right been merely hibernating in these four decades? Was the long postwar period just an incubation period? I will answer these questions separately for East and West.

There is relatively little known about what became of the rightist potential in the eastern part of Germany. We know that it was one of the highest government priorities to achieve a break with rightist traditions. There was probably nothing that had a higher taboo value in the GDR than anything that was associated with the rightist tradition in Germany. But alas, this attitude had little to do with critical discussion and debate. Overnight the population found itself on the side of the presumed victors of history, and that had as a consequence that things that weren't supposed to be couldn't be. The rightist tradition, which of course was no less virulent in this population than in the West, was outlawed by decree. This prohibition made any discussion superfluous. There is good reason to believe that this idea was destined to fail (apart from the fact that the ruling elite, not unlike their western counterparts, were soon willing to integrate functionaries of the old regime into the new one). In this nation of righteous believers, the right became an undiscussable topic—and thus was forced much more radically to go underground than in the West. In this way, one could argue, the right was better preserved. Indications are that old and new forms of right-wing radicalism continued to exist in the GDR (as was demonstrated by the Leipzig Institute for Youth Research) but were systematically suppressed. There were good reasons to believe that rightist traditions would survive in the GDR— precisely because right-wing radicalism had become a taboo topic in the GDR.

Things were quite different in western Germany. Here, too, for the first fifteen years right-wing radicalism was a tabooed topic. Here, too, debate and discussion failed to take place early on. Instead, the great majority threw itself into reconstruction. There is reason to believe that not insight but the steadily rising standard of living increasingly pulled the rug out from under the right. Moreover, in an epoch-making maneuver the CDU succeeded in integrating the rightist spectrum—with much greater success than any other European conservative parties had achieved. It managed to fragment right-wing groups by at times absorbing them and at times isolating them. Thus for decades there was no terrain for explicitly rightist and chauvinist parties. (A counterpart of this success is that with the diminishing cohesion of the Christian democrats, the CDU's ability to subvert the right is also in decline.) Thus the radical right in the west of Germany has less been defeated than absorbed. But because—unlike in the GDR—there was never a taboo, it then later became possible to conduct the debate that led all the way to the *Historikerstreit* of the eighties. The left and liberal side frequently points to the notorious German deficiency in taking on the past. This argument is not wrong, but it ignores the fact that over the years the debate about the past has not diminished—on the contrary, it has become more intensive.

Over decades the Federal Republic of Germany has been shaped by the stability of a party system that is unique in Europe. This stability has even come to be identified with the "nature" of the state. It seemed certain that the periods of precarious political majorities were long gone and that the right had been neutralized. Thus the public sphere reacted with all the more surprise to the election success of the NPD in the second half of the sixties, which for the first time presented the young republic with a (relatively small) economic setback. Back then, of course, there were more reasons to see this resurgence of the right as a revival of old rightist forces. In a large majority, these really were the old people who were acting out their nostalgia for the Third Reich or at least for radical authoritarianism. They would die off in the course of the years, and soon this spook, too, would disappear—this being the official line at the time. And indeed, after a brief period of election success the NPD experienced nothing but setbacks and eventually dropped out of all the state parliaments to which it had gained access. Only right-wing folklore seemed to survive.

That right-wing radicalism would not simply pass away was demonstrated by the famous (and methodologically problematic) Sinus demographic study of 1979–80, which caused a great uproar. According to this study, 13 percent of voters possessed a closed, right-wing extremist view of the world (hatred of foreigners, of democracy, and of pluralism; veneration of folk, family, and fatherland). And a good 37 percent demonstrated partial right-wing extremist opinions. In other words, half of the voters either had extreme rightist views or were sympathetic to such views. One aspect of this study was particularly disquieting: the fact that not only old people but also increasingly the young were susceptible to extreme rightist views.

But there was another disturbing thing. While the political right had in the past concerned itself with its traditional themes (the expulsion of Germans from eastern Europe, the division of Germany, etc.), new topics suddenly appeared, among them (from the beginning of the eighties) the theme of political asylum and applicants for political asylum. It is true that this, too, can be easily passed off as part of the right's political pattern of xenophobia, but it also represents a new aspect, because now the right took up the topic of a world growing together. This was, so to speak, a paradoxical success of leftist internationalism. By now the word had got around—even all the way to the right—that the world is marked by great injustice in the distribution of wealth and that the times are probably gone when the poor were willing to simply accept this. The thought that the "Third World" could come to our door (since wealth was unlikely to come to them) became a popular notion. For the first time one could experience for oneself that western Europe could no longer remain an island of prosperity. For the first time people also began to sense that there could be an end to the period of what seemed to be perpetual prosperity. It is important to note that the increase in asylum applicants was still quite small in the beginning of the eighties. But the right reacted to this with precision and vision when it noted that this was the fundamental conflict of the future, for which it recommended a response of resistance and sealing off the borders. The new version of right-wing radicalism used the language and emblems of the old one, but it developed genuinely new and current topics.

The early eighties were something like an incubation period for the new right-wing radicalism. Unlike in France, the new movement was without intellectual influence. Armin Mohler and Gert-Klaus Kaltenbrunner were still only capable of achieving the tiny majorities they were accustomed to because they insisted on remaining "old-fashioned" rightists (while the French right caused a stir with debates about ethnopluralism and the right to difference). On the other hand, rightism gradually increased its influence among young people. The first rock bands were calling attention to themselves with acts of right-wing provocation (so-called Oi music) and employed the old model, more familiar from the leftist scene, of transgressing against rules and taboos. This was (and is) a case of rebellious gestures being transposed into crude, uncouth, cruel, and barbarian dimensions. Parallel to that there existed a new system of radical rightist groups and sects. This system was (and is) shaped by rightist traditionalism, but it would be a mistake to overlook the fact that these groups have adopted elements of youth subcultures and appear to be supporters of a thoroughly modern aesthetic of the bizarre.

Not until the middle of the eighties, after the subcultural upsurge of the right, did the extreme right begin to organize and orient itself in political parties. In addition to the hopelessly old-fashioned NPD, the Republicans were founded. They and the DVU [Deutsche Volksunion or Union of German People, a political party] of Gerhard Frey initiated the first spectacular election success in Berlin and Bremen. By now it seemed beyond doubt that the extreme right would be able to establish itself in parliament—and at that moment, German-German unification plunged these groups into an existential crisis. For one thing, unification cost them their most important topic, and for another, unification had practical consequences that could not be masked using lofty nationalist rhetoric. The extreme right was less prepared for the German-German row about the small print and other material elements than were the others.

While the rightist parties had lost their appeal and had almost disappeared from public consciousness, right-wing violence "from below" continued to grow perceptibly, in the East as well as in the West. It appears that there were copycat patterns, with rightist violence spreading almost by capillary action. In 1992 about four thousand crimes against foreigners were registered, and half of them had a violent background. Seventeen people were killed, among them Captain Gustav Schneeclaus, whom skinheads beat to death because he called Hitler a criminal; the Vietnamese work-study student Nguyen Van Tu, who was stabbed to death on the street in the Marzahn section of Berlin; the Polish seasonal worker Ireneusz Szyderski, who was kicked to death by bouncers in a disco in Thuringia; Rolf Schulze, a homeless man who was murdered by skinheads who appear to have had no motive; and Bahide Arslan and Ayse Yilmaz, who on 23 November 1992 were burned to death in a midnight firebombing of a house lived in by Turks in Mölln.

These violent acts were all motivated by xenophobia. The victims were seen to deviate from some norm. In this respect, these barbaric acts have a common denominator. And a goal: to drive away or eliminate anyone who is "different" or who appears to be "different." At the same time, it is possible to note a strange lack of motive. Often the criminal cannot offer a trace of a motive. At times it seems to be violence for violence's sake— pure violence without goals and objectives. And in many cases rightist rhetoric and emblems appear merely as a disguise. This violence is an expression of a kind of brutalization, a peculiar mixture whose components, in the traditional logic of police work, appear to exclude each other: "authoritarian anti-authoritarianism" and "rebellious conformism" (Klaus Leggewie). No wonder, then, that more men than women are involved in these acts (even though women often have their role in the background). The great majority of violent offenders are young (under twenty) and not well organized; their political ideas are rudimentary; their reference to National Socialism is not encumbered by knowledge. In addition to these people, there are also organized and schooled groups that present a program—albeit a confused program— and that supply the key players in the rightist radical scene. It would certainly be wrong to portray the acts of these rightist violent offenders as being planned in advance. These are often spontaneous acts (even though the percentage of drunken offenders is lower than most people think), conducted without ringleaders. But it is important to keep in mind that an increasingly large number of assaults are planned. And it is usually remarkable (more in the East than in the West) that the firebombers can often operate with the agreement or even support of a substantial part of the population—Rostock-Lichtenhagen in August 1992 will remain a symbol of that.

According to a January 1993 report of the Hamburg Office for the Protection of the Constitution, there are in Germany today sixty-five thousand right-wing extremists (i.e., fewer than 0.1 percent of the overall population) of whom sixty-four hundred (10 percent) can be seen to be militant. About half of these sixty-four hundred militant right-wing extremists live in East Germany, in which only about one-quarter of the overall German population lives. One can only surmise that the number of people there who are susceptible to the lure of right-wing violent activism is greater. The problem is that these people are hard to identify and harder to recognize. Almost nowhere can we trace a direct route from social situation to crime. This violence leaves traces, but they are hard to follow. Claus Leggewie writes: "Whole squadrons of youth researchers have in the past years swarmed out into suburbs and the mass-constructed apartment developments in the East to try to find something that they could present as the solution to the riddle. But what they discovered was not social motivation, not even tangible social problems, but a black hole. A violent Nothing." And Georg Seeßlen emphasizes that this pointless violence is neither a revolt nor a reaction: "It neither anticipates a coming social order nor offers itself as a way of finding meaning. It fulfills neither traditions nor utopias; it is only habit and addiction. And because it disdains its victims, it offers no deliverance. It does not even function as a Nazi gesture." Neither revolt nor reaction: This indeed demonstrates that we are dealing with a new phenomenon that has yet to be interpreted and that perhaps will elude traditional forms of interpretation.

This is not to say that we should ignore the responsible parties and take flight into a nebulous, noncommittal attitude. There is no doubt of the fact that a significant part of the political class has attempted to instrumentalize the asylum question and thus has opened the floodgates of prudence and offered justification and impetus to those people who see political violence as a legitimate political means. The fact that in Rostock-Lichtenhagen a few hundred militant xenophobes succeeded in leading almost the entire political class around by the nose—that should not be forgotten.

2. THE EUROPEANS' FEAR OF CHANGE

Is this "new" form of "old" right-wing radicalism a specifically German phenomenon, a part of the German tradition, or is it a pan-European phenomenon that occurs in all parts of the continent? It is quite apparent that right-wing radicalism is a European phenomenon. That of course changes nothing of the fact that Germany always stands in a different context than other countries, nor of the fact that nowhere else in Europe does rightist violence occur in such a massive and blunt way.

Hans Magnus Enzensberger writes: "Xenophobia—a specifically German problem? That would not be too bad, no, it would be too good to be true. The solution is the obvious. One would just have to isolate the Federal Republic, and the rest of the world could breathe easier." But it cannot because it, too, is involved. How did this new wave of xenophobia and right-wing extremism arise in Europe?

Rightist parties had successes before 1989, but since that time, or so it would appear, they have been formulating a general sense of discontent more offensively than before. The end of the decades-long European prosperity phase was already evident and perceptible before 1989; thus since 1989, the year in which the Iron Curtain fell, the end of prosperity has become an inevitable certainty and for many a painful reality. Europe suddenly awoke from the dream of perpetual prosperity, and in such moments of sudden awakening there are always many who seek to lay blame and believe that they have found the culprits in the people that they consider to be foreign.

Just how ominous the new European disorder is becomes clear if we take the time to recall the prior historical phase. It was the period of the political order of Yalta. Its end was, with the fall of walls, a moment of unanticipated happiness, and in the more than forty years of the Cold War, the barbarism of the order of Yalta has been described countless times. But there was also another side (about which fewer people speak openly): The order of Yalta offered Europe, or at least western Europe, an unprecedented and unimaginable period of peace and prosperity. As absurd as this sounds, it is true. In the shadow of the bomb, western Europe experienced a phase of happiness singular in its history. Through the entire nineteenth century all the way until the end of World War II, Europe was engaged in perpetual strife about borders, and nationalism had given these disputes a particularly implacable character. Furthermore, capitalism had until that point been a model of crisis both in the peripheral countries and in the center of Europe. This historical background makes clear the fascination that emanated from the postwar order. First of all, the nuclear threat dictated there would be no more strife about borders. For the first time, western Europeans received the opportunity to come to know each other apart from battlefields. And for the first time they experienced a prosperity that had been unimaginable in the past.

Thus Europe profited from the order of Yalta. And one was inclined to declare it to be for the ages. That lulled citizens, parties, and governments in western Europe into the false conclusion that they had a surplus of time at their disposal. In this conviction western Europe neglected to use the "golden age of the Cold War" to resolutely advance European integration. Everything seemed headed for a postnational period, and the specters of the past seemed to have been exorcised. It seemed that it was just a matter of waiting. The astonishment and horror were then all the greater when suddenly there was no more time, when the order of Yalta had collapsed in the shortest imaginable time, and the specters of the past seemed to be returning in the form of ethnically motivated politics. No one was prepared for that. There was no stable postnational and integrated Europe that could have served as a model for eastern Europe. Suddenly the period of European nonhistory, the age of inaction in a quiet corner of world history, had passed.

Many traditionally conflict-rife themes that were without importance over the last decades suddenly became pressingly topical: the question about the national state and possible alternatives to it; the question of whether a united Europe would pose a danger for the tradition of European cultural difference; the question of how to deal with borders, in particular with open borders; and finally the question whether the prosperity that in western Europe had already attained the status of a fact of nature might in the long or short term be consigned to the past.

All the questions were posed before 1989, although in a hardly perceptible way. Prior to that the topic of poverty-motivated migration from the south of the world and from eastern Europe had been discussed with some virulence. In prior years there had also been questions about the European integration process and the fear that prosperity would decline. But for many people the epochal break of 1989 both made many of these presentments a certainty and furnished them with a new momentum. Increasingly, all these recent developments came to be viewed throughout Europe as a threat. What this has to do with xenophobia and right-wing radicalism is more than evident. Everyone knows that the golden age of constant growth has passed, and everyone knows that we in western Europe will have to learn something new: how to deal with crises in a civil, democratic way. But of course that also calls forth a specific reaction: the desire to hold on to what one has, the "every man for himself" mentality. Well equipped by the modern processes of individualization, many are reacting to the new, seemingly chaotic world with radical egotism and with greedy chauvinism. That leads to massive aggression against anyone who is perceived as threatening the attained level of wealth: the socially weaker people in one's own country as well as those who can be treated as socially inferior (since this kind of distinction permits the viewer to see himself as socially superior), and people who are foreign or can be perceived to be foreign—in a word, everyone who does not belong or who can be perceived as not belonging.

The arrival of immigrants has always caused a sense of discontent and hostility; this is no different in Germany than in France or the United States.

Immigration was always a sign that secure social relationships had begun to come apart or at least could be seen as coming apart. Immigrants are in a sense the messengers of the new indeterminacy and are repeatedly taken to be such messengers. Here, too, one result of the epoch-making shift of 1989 will also be increased East-West migration. And in all of western Europe there will be people who see the new migrants as the source of all the new problems. Right-wing radicalism, present in all of western Europe, is also an attempt to find culprits for the newly confused situation. It is important not to overlook the fact that the new rightist politics, aimed at ruthlessly preserving what we have, is attracting a great variety of actors and social groups: defenders of real as well as imaginary assets, subproletarian groups and the traditional skilled laborers who in the past were inclined toward social democracy.

Almost everywhere in Europe this mental shift to the right has had political consequences. Examples are familiar: the German "Republicans" and Le Pen's National Front in France; Jörg Heider's stormy successes in Austria as well as the success of right-wing separatist movements in Belgium that are openly fighting against the continuation of the Belgian nation. It is evident here that an old European conflict is being revived in the form of new rightist populism and right-wing radicalism: the conflict between universalism and particularism.

This can be recognized most clearly in the case of the Northern League in Italy, which makes it evident that we are dealing with a modern phenomenon, a modern particularism that has little to do with traditional right-wing programs. The Northern League is emphatically antinational; using the not-so-incorrect argument that one hundred years of national unity had offered the south few opportunities for development and had harmed the north, the league propagates (or has propagated) the end of Italy's attempt to create a stable national state. The Northern League, hardly a catch-basin for people who live only in the past, is a movement aimed at protecting ownership. The wealthy north desires to break away from the middle and especially from the poor south and to seek linkage to prosperous northern Europe. The Northern League unifies a strange mixture: Xenophobia is as much a part of its program as is federalism, in which case this group—and not the brutish, backwards-oriented right-wing extremism of the "Republicans"—could be an indicator organization.

It is certain that the rightist renaissance in Germany is a part of a pan-European upsurge of the right, an upsurge that began in the West and has spread to the East. And in a sense, this rightist renaissance is a return to normalcy for Germany. To prevent possible misunderstandings: This is not an attempt to portray rightist extremism as legitimate. I am merely pointing out the fact that all modern societies call forth movements dedicated to antimodernity, and there is no reason to assume that Germany of all countries should be an exception to this rule. For the rightist renaissance is also a consequence of the fact that traditional parties, groups, and associations have lost their cohesive force. To overstate the case: The new, near-universal shift in values that has been welcomed by all sides has also helped the extreme right. (Incidentally, if it is true that the renaissance of the extreme right is an expression of normalization, then nothing speaks for fighting against the parliamentary part of the right by seeking to isolate them. If, and this appears to be the case, right-wing extremist views are widespread, then we have little chance of changing them if we ignore them or engage in the magical practice of denial. Only offensive, public dispute can have an effect. Isolation policies just confirm right-wing voters' conviction that they have been isolated all along.)

3. HARMFUL CONSEQUENCES OF UNIFICATION

Even if new forms of old right-wing radicalism are a pan-European phenomenon, they have taken on a particularly frightening face in Germany. Nowhere else in Europe is the road from right-wing extreme opinion to right-wing extreme act so direct and so short as in Germany. And nowhere else have the barriers of civilized behavior fallen so massively and quickly as in Germany. Nowhere else have rightist mobs taken the stage as aggressively and self-confidently as in Germany.

There are no doubt numerous reasons for this. For one thing, this may have to do with the tenacious survival of rightist dispositions from the past. Forty years of democracy, as we are now seeing, is not that much. These years have apparently not been sufficient to provide a truly stable anchor for democracy. Add to this the process of German-German unification that has presented democracy in Germany with another test: German society has grown by seventeen million new citizens who possess no experience with democratic structures, rights, and obligations. Now, in the newly sovereign Germany that is no longer subject to external discipline, we will see if democracy and the adherence to the values of the liberal West are really solidly anchored or if they only endured as long as what appeared to be perpetual prosperity was not seriously challenged. The actions of a large part of the political class give reason for doubt. Many of these politicians have quite obviously lost their sense of orientation since unification. The populist use of the asylum problem and the—to put it mildly—mindless reaction of numerous prominent politicians to the excesses of Rostock-Lichtenhagen have given reason to doubt whether the political class of the republic (in particular its younger members) will hold fast to democracy and democratic rules in times of crisis.

It has been repeatedly debated whether this new right-wing radicalism is stronger in the new or the old states. There is no doubt that more crimes of this type are committed in the West than in the East—the West, after all, is four times as large as the East. But in truth there are more important things than numerical comparisons. Of greater importance is the question: Which part of Germany is more susceptible to right-wing radicalism? This is not a question of numbers but of the character of the social environment in both parts of the country. And here the great difference between East and West Germany becomes visible.

The west of Germany, the "old" Federal Republic, possesses a political and democratic self-confidence that has grown over the decades. It also possesses a fairly stable system of rules and a public sphere that by and large makes sure that these rules are adhered to. The problem is not the absolute number of rightist radicals. Extreme rightists, xenophobes, and aggressive people exist in all societies. The question should be: What degree of self-confidence, what strength, what degree of self-assurance does democratic society possess in its dealings with its enemies? Can it be made insecure by antidemocratic impulses? Do the rules of decency have authoritative character? Viewed in this way, the differences between West Germany and East Germany are quite apparent.

On the one side is the western part of Germany, the "old" Federal Republic. It drew the longer straw. Even if its residents at first resisted, it succeeded in linking itself to the traditions of Western democracy and became the first German state in which democracy really found acceptance. There is no doubt that the people who really founded this democracy, especially Konrad Adenauer, the first chancellor of the republic, had in mind anything but a libertarian state based on dissent. But the founders laid a foundation for just this kind of state whose democracy later generations, especially the one of 1968, accepted in dissent. The Federal Republic of Germany became the first German state in which democracy was not the hated exception but the welcome rule.

And on the other side there was the German Democratic Republic, a state without legitimacy, without a real public sphere; a state whose residents had lived under continuing dictatorship since 1933—i.e., for more than a half century; a state that prescribed friendship with other peoples but also made contact with these peoples almost impossible for its citizens; a state that made antifascism a doctrine of state and in this way placed its citizens on the side of the victors with a stroke of the pen, exculpating them for all that had happened. For obvious reasons, all this had few civilizing effects. The GDR remained the older, the more German state. Without wanting to overtax the metaphor: Old mentalities remained frozen in the ice of socialism, and now they are reemerging in malignant innocence. A part of this pernicious thinking holds that Germany belongs to the Germans—a conviction that has received additional impetus from the shock of unification and its consequences. This can explain why xenophobia has the stronger force in eastern Germany and why resentment is easier to stoke up there. We will see if West Germany can stand up to this test and whether it can expand and buttress its civic self-definition, or whether it can be subverted by the disintegration of values that has taken place in the East.

There is an additional problem: The Germans do not like each other. This does not stem from the recent time at which the Germans were unified in one state. The unification of the states just updated old domestic strife that has a long tradition. In a word: Nothing in the many-faceted and unclear contours of German history indicates the necessity or even the potential for a national state. That is a result of the federalist tradition in Germany, of German regionalism, and of German obstinance. Because there is no homogeneous German nation and because in the decisive period in which the state was constituted in the nineteenth century there was no political concept of state and community, the German state was founded on a concept of ethnicity. So a German is defined as a person with German blood. In the seventy-five years of its existence this nation-state has brought the Germans and the rest of the world little happiness. One particular aspect of this history is of interest here: The national state did not make the Germans, who did not particularly care for each other, any more intimate with each other, because there was no foundation for a unifying sense of community. Under the fictitious mantle of the nation, the old sense of estrangement lived on. So did the domestic tradition of an east-west gradient in economic levels, which was not created by the Iron Curtain but was accentuated more clearly by it. Now Germans and Germans are united despite the fact that they are strangers to each other and that they are now experiencing that unity, rather than unifying us, can cause separation. Now we have what political speeches have demanded over decades, and we see that unification (if it was ever really desired) has far from produced the happiness all longed for. And thus begins, not surprisingly, the old German quarrel, the old inner-German strife, anew. And it certainly contains the potential for a shift to the right.

4. NEW OR OLD RIGHT-WING RADICALISM?

Many factors seem to indicate that today's rampant right-wing radicalism is clearly distinct from the rightist extremism of the thirties. It lacks a clearly defined goal; all the arguments it can produce sound like pretenses and masquerade. The movement comes (as the recent documentation from the Federal Ministry for Women and Youth has shown) from the margins as well as the center of society—as much from marginalized people as from those who appear to be normal. Despite all attempts to explain right-wing radical violence as a product of its social causes, the rule that is characteristic for this right-wing radicalism is that it cannot be explained socially. "Germany for the Germans!" "Out with the foreigners!" Slogans like these express less a program than an aggressive feeling. Right-wing radicalism is also a product of what could be called the "extreme normality" of this society. Boredom and satiety play a bigger role here than real problems. This gives expression to a social implosion, not an explosion, which originates, to an extent, in the center of society.

Its radical denial of reason and its self-justifications put a society that is adept at finding justifications to a difficult test. And the new movement must be viewed as an attempt to create communities at a time in which it is difficult to create communities without justifying them. To this extent the movement is—even if it would deny it—a product of the shift in values and the pluralization of life-styles. It also profits from the decline of political certainties. The agonized political impulse that has been the dominant experience for two hundred years only finds expression from the right wing of the spectrum. And to the extent that the large parties do not succeed in attracting the middle, i.e., the great number of little people, right-wing radicalism will lay claim to being the movement of these little people. Rightist extremism is always most successful where a shift in values fails to create new forms of cohesion and is thus experienced as diffusion and stress.

Hans Magnus Enzensberger has spoken of a "molecular civil war" that has long since become reality. And, he adds, it is apparent that universalism has become a dull weapon in the struggle against violence. I think it would be a mistake to put the old conflict between universalism and particularism on the agenda in this way. It is true that universalism is still important, but we need a universalism that is capable of making space for particularism. As American philosopher Michael Walzer has formulated it: "If I can feel secure I will acquire a more complex identity than the ideas of particularism allow for. I will then identify with more than one group: I'll be an American, a Jew, a resident of the East Coast, an intellectual, and a professor. Now try to imagine a similar multiplication of identities everywhere in the world, and the world begins to look a little less dangerous. If identities can multiply, passions are often shared."

LITERATURE

Thomas Assheuer and Hans Sarkovics, *Rechtsradikale in Deutschland. Die alte und die neue Rechte* (Munich, 1992).
Hans Magnus Enzensberger, *Die Große Wanderung. 33 Markierungen* (Frankfurt/ Main, 1992).

————, "Ausblicke auf den Bürgerkrieg," *Der Spiegel,* no. 25 (1993): 170–75.

Klaus Farin and Eberhard Seidel Pielen, *Rechtsruck. Rassismus im neuen Deutschland* (Berlin, 1992).

Wilhelm Heitmeyer et al., *Die Bielefelder Rechtsextremismus-Studie* (Weinheim and Munich, 1992).

Claus Leggewie, *Druck von rechts. Wohin treibt die Bundesrepublik?* (Munich, 1993).

Sinus, *Die verunsicherte Generation* (Opladen, 1983).

Michael Walzer, "Das neue Stammeswesen," *Zivile Gesellschaft und amerikanische Demokratie* (Berlin, 1992).

Helmut Willems et al., *Fremdenfeindliche Gewalt: Eine Analyse von Täterstrukturen und Eskalationsprozessen* (Bonn, June 1993) (Dokumentation des Bundesministeriums für Frauen und Jugend).

6

FOREIGNERS—TODAY'S JEWS? XENOPHOBIC RIGHT-WING RADICALISM AND THE FUNDAMENTALISM OF THE OTHER

BASSAM TIBI

Speaking about right-wing radicalism in German history means dealing with the political culture of Germany and with the evident stresses on German democracy. It is not by coincidence that I introduce this publication and the lecture on which it is based with some thoughts on anti-Semitism and conclude them with thoughts about xenophobia. In comparing anti-Semitism and xenophobia as forms of right-wing radicalism in our crisis-ridden time, we run up against a number of problems. On the one hand, it seems to me that this parallel is based on a false footing, as I will attempt to point out. On the other hand, as a foreigner who has grown up in German culture, as a German foreigner, I would like to stress my observation that the German fear of strangers does not necessarily qualify as xenophobia and thus cannot necessarily be classified as right-wing radicalism. The xenophobia that is actually present in Germany and that is based on limited right-wing xeno-phobia, and the inability of Germans to deal with things and people alien to them, seem to me to be two quite distinct phenomena. The first is associ-ated with right-wing radicalism, while the second results from the fact that the Germans at best know the world outside of their country as tourists and, in contrast to their European neighbors, have had no experience with other, alien cultures. In the political culture of Germany one can observe much provincialism, which, however, is not the same as xenophobia.

The political thinker who desires to gain orientation from recent history and who, in the aftermath of Rostock, Solingen, and other such events, studies the excesses of German right-wing extremists against foreigners must begin his undertaking with the question of whether the foreigners living in Germany today have become the objects of what Georg Lukacs once called "peculiarities of the historical development of Germany."[1] One of these peculiarities is the Germans' aversion toward everything that seems alien to them. I am not formulating this sentence as a prejudgment but as a result of my thirty years' experience of living among the Germans. In other words: I want to criticize the inability of the Germans to deal with things alien to them, but I also want to protect them from a blanket incrimination as "xenophobes." If I link this finding to the task given to me by my publisher, Ernst Reinhard Piper, then I would have to conclude—with apparent logic— that foreigners have taken over the position that the Jews once occupied for the Germans. Yet I consider this intimated equation to be wrong, as I argued in "False Parallels," my recent article in the *Frankfurter allgemeine Zeitung*.[2] Writing about this topic in a critical time in which new fronts are being formed and seeking to make differentiations means running the risk of ending up between the fronts. My criticism of the Germans could be misunderstood as anti-German just as my rejection of any blanket incrimination of the Germans as "xenophobes" could be misunderstood as playing down right-wing xenophobia. It is important for me to emphasize that I am free of the guilt complexes of many a "high-minded" German and thus do not feel compelled to cleanse myself of xenophobia with the help of xenophilia. I will not spare foreigners in my criticism of right-wing radicalism, because I also see a right-wing radical danger to democracy in the fundamentalism that is widespread in parts of the Islamic community in Germany.

This study consists of two parts. In the first part I concern myself with the Germans, while the focus of the second part is on a concrete community among the foreigners who live in Germany: the Muslims. Beyond all guilt complexes and "high-mindedness," rightist radicalism can be found on both sides, and in both cases it represents a danger for democracy in Germany. Thus in this context I make demands not only of the Germans but also of the foreigners who live in Germany.

1. Two Different Objects: Anti-Semitism and Xenophobia

At first I would like to stress that anti-Semitism is a pan-European phenomenon, even if the Germans did develop this malaise all the way to the barbarities of National Socialism. As a foreigner coming from the Islamic Orient and a person who has appropriated Cartesian thought in the tradition of German idealism and the Frankfurt school that rests upon it, I am a persistent critic of the Germans; but I am also a man who has learned to think in the traditions of modernism and who loves the democratic traits of German culture.[3] Like many of my Jewish friends, from my dear deceased friend Reinhard Bendix to Shlomo Avineri, who teaches in Jerusalem, to my Jewish teachers of the Frankfurt school, I am indebted to German culture and refuse—despite harsh criticism—to engage in making a bogeyman of the Germans. It is very strange to find myself again in situations where I have to use Enlightenment positions to defend German culture against its romanticizing German self-haters. Later I will elucidate why my fear of anti-Western German romanticism-as-counter-Enlightenment is no smaller than my fear of German xenophobia.

The Germany that I love is the Germany of Western culture. Many a contemporary German intellectual's hatred of the West (the Gulf War offers an example), linked to a revival of German anti-Western romanticism, not only awakens my fear of some Germans, whom Jews and foreigners cannot fully trust.[4] It is obvious that the German contribution to the Western Enlightenment, i.e., those components of German culture that have inspired me and other like-thinking democratic foreigners and Jews, has yet to become a key trait of German political culture. The Germans have been marked by the "particularity" of their history to which German political culture "owes its estrangement from the Western spirit" (Habermas). As a people, the Germans are still today peculiar and fearful and in our context hostile to that which is alien to them. The activation of this "peculiarity" (Lukacs) in our time evokes fear in me. In a book edited by Kurdish writer Namo Aziz I describe this feeling in an essay entitled "Not via Baghdad but Directly: The Difficulty of Feeling at Home at a German University."[5] A German nationalist would respond to this kind of formulation by aggressively asking: Then why don't you leave Germany? This question was asked to me right after the Munich lecture. After the Gulf War I had responded to this kind of question in my talk "What Do the Germans Think?" that I presented at Frankfurt's Church of St. Paul in the framework of the symposium "When I Think of Germany."[6] The symposium's title comes from the Jewish thinker Heine, who is clearly a participant in German culture. As a German foreigner I want to live in this country in the framework of Heine's cultural heritage. For me, Heine is a part of the German democratic culture that unfortunately remained peripheral until 1945. After the taming of German fascism—by the very West against which many a German is demonstrating today—a process of westernization and thus democratization began. The reduction of anti-Semitism and xenophobia is a part of this process by which Germany is being integrated into Western political culture and on which

German Jews and foreigners and German democrats have been working ever since. Has Germany succeeded in this process? Is Germany today a different, a more westernized democratic Germany? These are questions we must ask ourselves if we want to speak about new and old right-wing radicalism.

Before I get into this substantive question I would like to emphasize that as a German foreigner I distinguish between western and eastern Germany, without wanting to participate in the "Ossi-Wessi" polemic current among Germans. That is none of my business. As a German foreigner I am more afraid of East Germans, who are much more likely to embody the peculiarities of German history than the West Germans, who have been at least partially integrated into Western culture. For this reason I am not surprised when many observers conclude that there is a greater Nazi potential in the East than in the West, be it in the form of anti-Semitism or in the form of xenophobia. For me this is a proof that the democratic potential present in the western part of Germany is a result of the democratization coming from the West. Eastern Germany still has a need to catch up in regard to democratization and internalizing democratic values—to put it as frankly as I can.

I would now like to move to the question of what has happened in Germany since 1945 and whether the desired change has taken place. A Jerusalem experience in a Jewish setting but with a non-Jewish speaker will illustrate what I mean.

In a public lecture series at the renowned Israeli Van Leer Foundation in Jerusalem in early January of 1993, a Gypsy living in Germany gave a talk in which he offered answers to our questions. Without beating around the bush he compared the Federal Republic and the Third Reich in order to support his thesis that "nothing has changed in Germany since 1945." He accused the Federal Republic of denying Gypsies in Germany what it was demanding for the Volga-Germans in Russia: autonomy. The Gypsy repeatedly and wordily invoked the comparison of xenophobia and anti-Semitism that I cast doubt upon in my introduction. Sitting next to me was Shlomo Avineri, a prominent Israeli political scientist specializing in Germany. He described the talk as "propaganda," an assessment that unfortunately not all the people present shared—many of them were older and had suffered at the hands of the Germans. Shlomo Avineri, who has written a book about Hegel, knows from his own experience that the Federal Republic is a democratic society.[7] In light of this fact it is unfortunate that this ideological comparison is being employed by many a "high-minded" German publicist to support his moralizing self-accusations. Yet we have still to answer the question I asked in the beginning: whether both phenomena—the anti-Semitism and xenophobia of the Germans—are in fact comparable. This question should lead to another: Would founding ethnic collectives within German society, as they were demanded by the cited Gypsy speaker, be a contribution to democratizing Germany, to both reducing and overcoming anti-Semitism and xenophobia?

I would like to anticipate my thoughts in the second part of this essay by saying that founding foreign ethnic collectives in Germany would be more likely to increase xenophobia. I would like to introduce the following thoughts with the observation that both of these objects, anti-Semitism and xenophobia, have only one thing in common: Both cause stress on the young, Western-inspired German democracy. The content of most of the other elements of this comparison is also far-fetched. The Jews are a people, and the Germans owe them historical reconciliation. But there is no nationality such as "foreigners." Young German democracy can demonstrate that it has achieved much toward overcoming anti-Semitism, as the deceased Jewish scholar Reinhard Bendix (author of *From Berlin to Berkeley*) repeatedly pointed out.[8] Michael Wolffsohn, a German Jew and an author of the Piper Verlag, called one of his books *No Fear of Germany* in order to laud this achievement—despite many a reservation he has.[9] Just as German Jews are a part of German culture, foreigners who live in Germany have, as German foreigners, played a role in the young history of German democracy. In the Church of St. Paul in Frankfurt I said in April 1991 that there were reasons to see this integration of non-Germans in Germany as a component or as an offshoot of German democracy. I said: "Ethnically I am a non-German, but culturally I am a German . . . despite the rejection I experience. And I hope that I will succeed in accounting for . . . this tradition of German democracy."[10] In contrast to the Jews as a people, there is no clearly defined entity "foreigner" for the Germans to relate to. There is no clearly constituted entity, no ethnic group by this name. Thus I suggest uncoupling German foreigners as a group and their concerns from the rest of mankind, who from the German perspective are also foreigners. Only in this way can we seriously discuss the topic of German foreigners. In coming to grips with the topic of German foreigners we are dealing not with misery or political persecution outside of the country but concretely with foreigners who live in Germany. It is very important to keep these two realms separate.

In the West German debate, pro-asylum groups have used the term "xenophobia" in a nonspecified way in order to point an accusing finger at the German politicians who suggest that it is necessary to limit immigration to the Federal Republic since the country cannot be open to everyone who would like to move here. In this context it is wrong to incriminate the anxieties of the German population who fear the social consequences of unlimited immigration by calling these people xenophobes or racists.[11] In the large German cities like Frankfurt, Munich, and Hamburg, Germans and foreigners lived next to each other in peace before the great influx of immigrants began. I would like to use the term "German foreigner" for those foreigners who are integrated into German society. German foreigners are thus people who live this country as the homeland of their choice, who want to contribute to the country's well-being by their achievements, and who above all express an allegiance to the country's democracy. The integration of these German foreigners into the democratic German community, in which they can become citizens, would be a contribution to consolidating young German democracy. By contrast, forming ethic collectives in the framework of uncontrolled immigration would substantially impede German democracy. The group comprised of German foreigners is distinct from the millions of people in the world who—based on my observations during many trips around the world—are waiting with packed bags to come to the promised "Paradise Germany," aided by organized gangs of smugglers. These are largely people from premodern cultures. There is no fundamental right to immigration. One should not confuse the human dignity of these "foreigners" and their calls for help with a right to immigration.

The wish by a majority of Germans to limit immigration should not be viewed as being identical to xenophobia. The German fear of what is alien cannot be overcome by prescribing an exaggerated "xenophilia" based on ethical considerations, nor is it helped by self-accusation. Germans can only overcome their fear by day-to-day contact with the foreigners who live in Germany, who make their home here, and who are integrated as democratic fellow citizens. Xenophobia, which does exist as a clear potential here, can only be mastered concretely with the German foreigners who have achieved rights through their contributions to the German community.

"Noble-minded" spokesmen for the unlimited opening of the borders support immigration and accuse their critics of xenophobia. But they are conflating xenophobia with the German population's fear of the consequences of such immigration, i.e., the formation of ethnic, nonintegrated, marginalized groups and the predictable social consequences. By contrast, even the integrated foreigners living in Germany know that the Germans have problems with that which is alien to them. Thus they do not confuse this with the xenophobia that is present among right-wing radicals. For this reason one must—critically—defend the German population from the blanket incrimination that unfortunately has become fashionable in the media. According to my own observations, foreign media pick up the image Germans project of themselves in the media here and spread it internationally as "facts." This is bad for the democratic reputation of Germany and for its political and economic relations with other nations.

Uncontrolled immigration could, viewed from the perspective I have described, endanger the integration into German society of the foreigners who are already living in Germany while at the same time contributing to the formation of ethnic-based marginalized groups, who for their part might reinforce the xenophobic potential in this society. Any community that consists of nonintegrated collectives will be troubled with the problem of ethnicity. Violent conflicts are the result. Globally, ethnicity seems to be on the way to becoming the chief source of conflict in the transition to the twenty-first century.[12] Pointing out the fears of these German, i.e., integrated, foreigners is neither xenophobia nor self-hatred, as I argued in a letter to the editor of the *Frankfurter allgemeine Zeitung* that was discussed nationwide.[13] For its well-being, every society needs a population that has been integrated into the framework of its political culture to form a community. Thus the demand that foreigners who are to live in Germany should be integrated is neither "Germanization" (Heiner Geißler) nor an arrogant or xenophobic attitude aimed at these foreigners. As I will show in the section about Muslims in a European Germany, integration means nothing more than acknowledging cultural modernism and its democratic political culture. Europeans cannot do without this unless they want to endanger the cultural identity of Europe. Like other societies, Germany possesses a limited capacity for integration. Thus this influx of immigrants must be limited—not cut off. Failing to achieve this represents neither a contribution to the wellbeing of foreigners living in Germany nor a step against xenophobia. In this kind of situation, ethnic collectives of foreigners would summon up the collective of German right-wing radicals from the counterfront. Democracy would suffer—as would Germans and foreigners who see themselves as democratic individuals and not members of collectives. Of course it would be possible to develop "high-minded" arguments against this kind of scenario. But such "high-mindedness" hardly provides the basis to construct a reality-oriented social option that would encourage using a pluralistic political culture to master the Germans' historically and culturally conditioned inability to deal with things and people alien to them.

Just as there are German Jews such as Walter Grab who, despite all understandable distance, are obligated to German culture, young German democracy has also generated a tradition of German foreigners. Germany is the chosen home of these German foreigners, many of whom have children who are undeniably a part of Germany. These "German foreigners" should be distinguished from people who have no relationship to Germany. Integrating the foreigners living in Germany is one problem, and the misery of this world (poverty and persecution) is quite another. The two things should not be confused. Everywhere in this world there are economic misery and political persecution. Many of these people living abroad want to immigrate to Europe. European democracies are, in the words that Max Horkheimer, the Jewish father of the Frankfurt school, wrote shortly before his death "at the moment still an island, temporally and spatially, whose demise in an ocean of violence would mean the demise of culture."[14] Since Horkheimer wrote these words in 1968, this polarization has increased significantly. Since the end of the Cold War there has been an increase of misery and violence outside of this hemisphere. The West assumes a humane perspective in mastering its problems. But can Europe or little Germany solve all these problems by opening its borders to unlimited immigration from these worldwide areas of misery and terror? If we do not put a stop to the current migration, we will gradually destroy the democratic community of Europe while failing to reduce the increasing polarization between immigrants from premodern cultures and the European core population.

Many Germans, conditioned by the encumbrance of their past, feel inhibited when they speak about these problems. Similar to the Jewish historian Walter Grab or the Jewish sociologist Reinhard Bendix, who as participants in German culture are able to speak about German culture in a historically uninhibited way, German foreigners can also think aloud and without inhibitions about practical means and methods to overcome xenophobia in Germany and to limit immigration. German "high-minded" ethics, which Helmut Plessner in his emigration years after fleeing Nazi dictatorship called "inner-worldly piousness," knows only one solution: Xenophilia is the medicine against xenophobia. Helmut Plessner wrote, lamenting "high-minded" German ethical systems: "In public matters we Germans do not know how to find a proper balance and thus always fall victim to the magic of extreme deification of the state or extreme denial of the state."[15] The same can be said for the problem of foreigners. In the public life of the Federal Republic one can find extreme love of foreigners existing next to xenophobia. A precondition for an unproblematic relationship to foreigners is always loving one's self. A German who hates himself and his country can certainly not love me as a foreigner. Just as philo-Semitism is an expression of unmastered anti-Semitism, an excessive love of foreigners is only an expression of unmastered xenophobia.[16]

Referring to Theodor Adorno, who in American exile used American objects and his German background to develop his concept of the "authoritarian personality," we can get a grasp on the German inclination toward extremes and place the psychological mechanisms of xenophobia and xenophilia on the same stage of authoritarian extremism.[17] When the potential victims of xenophobia, the German foreigners, warn against excessive love of foreigners, they are accused by many a "high-minded" German of engaging in self-hatred (see F. Niewöhner's letter to the *Frankfurter allgemeine Zeitung* of 29 December 1992 in response to my letter cited in note 13). German foreigners who are not self-haters and who fear for their integration demand concrete recognition and not "high-minded" xenophilia. For only if Germans here and now master their fear of things alien can they help German foreigners in their lives in Germany. Germans can only prove their good intentions with the foreigners who live in their country.

German foreigners know as well as Jews that immigration in the past and the present are not the cause of xenophobia and anti-Semitism. But immigration can dramatically aggravate an already existing potential. Jewish historian Abraham Léon has shown how nineteenth-century migration from eastern Europe considerably inflamed existing anti-Semitism.[18] In this context it would be to scorn the Jewish victims of German anti-Semitism if we were to place them on the same level as emigrants who have been smuggled in from poor countries for a high payment to gangs. Eastern European Jews were fleeing pogroms, while today's immigrants from the East and the Mediterranean area, the victims of smuggler gangs, are fleeing from economic misery in the hope of getting to the "German Paradise" for a cash payment. These two cases cannot be compared morally. My Jewish friends see this comparison as an attempt—intended or not—to trivialize Nazi crimes.

The German discussion about xenophobia, inspired by the excesses of 1992, can make a significant contribution to German democracy. I would suggest shifting this discussion away from an ethic based on "high-minded," even narcissistic ideals to an ethic based on practical responsibility. That would concretely mean moving away from platitudes and expressions of dogma toward seeking to differentiate. In my introduction, which criticized the Germans, I found the parallel between anti-Semitism and xenophobia to be unfounded. In fact every non-German is a foreigner. This notion of German xenophobia would intimate constructing a German front against the rest of mankind. And that kind of suggestion is not a serious basis for a fruitful discussion.

In brief: When we speak of xenophobia, we are talking about the foreigners who live in Germany, not mankind in general. The German problems with foreigners can only be mastered if they are understood on this level—and not based on "high-minded" ethical laments about poverty and misery in the whole world. Furthermore, the foreigners living in Germany—in contrast to the rather homogeneous group of the Jews—come from numerous cultures. Thus these problems have to be tackled concretely and with reference to specific cultures. In the second section I would like to concentrate on the numerically largest group among the foreigners living in Germany, the Muslim immigrants, to further develop and discuss the questions I have already posed.

2. GERMANS AND MUSLIMS: ISLAMIC IMMIGRANTS AND THE RELIGIOUS INTEGRATION OF ISLAM IN EUROPE. TOWARD OVERCOMING RIGHT-WING RADICALISM ON BOTH SIDES

Talking about xenophobia in Germany in the context of a discussion about right-wing radicalism should not degenerate to a one-sided attack on the

Germans! Right-wing radicalism also exists among the victims of German xenophobia. Foreign right-wing radicals should not be exempted from critical reflection just because they are foreigners, in other words, potential victims. In my introduction I said how difficult it was to write about this sensitive subject in a crisis-ridden time without permitting taboos to influence the discussion. Also in my introduction, I broke one of the taboos when I noted that among the Muslims living in Germany (they make up one-third of the foreign population) there are fundamentalists that any normal observer would classify as members of the right-wing radical scene. In other words, when we engage in the necessary discussion of German xenophobia as a form of right-wing radicalism, we must be careful to include a parallel discussion about Islamic fundamentalism as a variant of totalitarianism. How does the democratic system of the Federal Republic react to immigration and to the fact that immigration in part comes from premodern cultures that know no democracy? Is there a concept for integrating these immigrants into German culture? If we speak of integrating the foreigners who are living in this country, then we must examine the political systems from which they come. For this reason I would like to preface my thoughts for this second section with the statement: Among European political systems, that of the Federal Republic stands out as the most cumbersome in its adaptation to the conditions of political change. While neighboring European nations have been quickly able to change their systems to the extent that they have recognized that Europe has become the goal of mass migration—that a massive, worldwide migration is heading for Europe—the Germans have for years, until the change in the Basic Law in 1993, been discussing political asylum. Politicians refuse to admit that immigration is happening; they fail to recognize that this can only be regulated by an immigration law. As a Muslim who rejects the Sharia in its present form, I can hardly suppress the comparison that occurs to me when I think of the legalism of the Germans and that of the Sharia. Interest, or *riba*, is forbidden in Islam, but in Islamic history there have always been interest rate increases. Muslims refer to the norm that forbids interest as a form of reality-denial. German jurists argue in a similar way: Legally, Germany is not a country of immigration. But immigration is taking place every day. Because that does not exist legally, it cannot exist in reality. Is there not a similarity between this German legalism and the rigidity of Islamic Sharia? Islamic fundamentalists do not exclude the Federal Republic in their demand to apply the Sharia. Like the other European countries, the Federal Republic cannot solve the problems of the economic misery in this world by opening its borders to unlimited immigration. Nor can one country alleviate the problems of political persecution by unlimited acceptance of asylum seekers. Recently the French and Americans set new legal standards here.[19] In order to protect its own system from collapse, each country has to create quotas for immigration and political asylum. All prognoses suggest that a massive influx from the southern Mediterranean countries is on the horizon (population growth prognosis for 2015: 270 million people in the Islamic Mediterranean countries in contrast to 127 million in the EU nations that border on the Mediterranean).[20] The main influx is currently coming from eastern Europe, but experts say this is a temporary phenomenon.

Immigration from the Mediterranean will exacerbate the consequences of massive migration because it will come from Islamic countries where at the moment Islamic fundamentalism is on the rise. Thus in addition to the problems it will cause labor market integration, there will be the problem of integrating Islam in Europe. The problem is that this religious community—according to the Koran (6:110)—claims exclusivity and superiority over all other religions. The acts of Islamic fundamentalists often promote a hostile image of Islam among Europeans (for example: an Islamic counterparliament in London in early January 1992)[21] that stands in the way of integration. The problems also come from the Muslims themselves. Here we must carefully consider that Islam is not identical with fundamentalism. Islam is an ancient world religion, while fundamentalism is a totalitarian ideology.[22]

Among the Europeans the French seem to possess the most experience in this area. The Germans can learn much from them. In contrast to here in the Federal Republic, France has already made the sobering experience that massive immigration is taking place in Europe. There, too, the related problems of sociocultural, political, and economic integration are being discussed in a taboo-free way. In Paris this problem is considered to be one of European policy and thus not limited to France.[23] The difference between Germany and France is one between a Western country with a long democratic tradition and one that is still engaged in the process of westernization—whereby resistance against forming democratic culture today comes equally from the left and the right. It is comforting to note the French lack of moralizing and "high-minded" utterances such as are regularly heard in the Federal Republic. In Paris one objectively considers that migration processes are happening and that as a consequence integration problems will arise that must be managed democratically.

For the French, Islam is in the center of the immigration question because a large portion of the immigrants come from the world of Islam. This will soon, once the migration from eastern Europe has been normalized, be the case in Germany, too. The migrants from the Mediterranean area have Islam as a political and cultural reference point of their identity. The French see this problem pragmatically, which means that for them the migrants in Europe are a social fact in the sociological sense of a *fait social*. In the same way the French quickly move to the question of how Europe can integrate

Muslim immigrants. This question receives its orientation from the two existing options for the Muslims in Europe: Will they be integrated into democratic culture, i.e., will they accept the three fundamental principles of European modernism that shape all western European societies? Or will they be a European Daar al-Islam (House of Islam) and remain unintegrated? In this context the most important principles of European democracy as a political culture are easy to describe; they are (1) pluralism; (2) tolerance as a concept of the Enlightenment in the sense of cultural modernism—which does not include what the Muslims understand by tolerance, such as "tolerating Christians and Jews as wards" (*dhimmi*). Rather, the European notion includes a sense of tolerating people who disagree; (3) secularism (in France this secularism is a component of political culture), which means the separation of politics and religion. In Paris I coined the term "Euro-Islam or ghetto-Islam" for the self-exclusionary options of Muslims in Europe.[24]

If the Muslims who live in Europe accept these basic principles of European modernism, then they can become an integrated religious community consisting of individuals as free citizens (not an *umma* collective). This community could then be a model for their home countries. Euro-Muslims, i.e., integrated individuals living in Europe in a democratic community as free citizens, could then, by appropriating the enlightenment of cultural modernism, become outposts of liberal reform and democracy in the relations between the Orient and the Occident. Otherwise there will be a danger that the extremists among them will use European democracy to transform Islamic centers in Europe into spearheads of fundamentalism. There are already examples of this. The spread of Islamic fundamentalism among the Islamic migrants in Europe would be suited to inflame European fears of Islam and to evoke hostile images. It is remarkable that the mere mention of this problem is misinterpreted by "high-minded" Germans as an attempt to establish a hostile image of Islam. Islamic fundamentalism is anti-Western and can count on support from anti-Western romanticism. This kind of alliance would be deadly for German democracy.[25]

Moralizing and high-minded ethics are of no use with this hot topic. A realistic political concept is needed in Europe. In light of my introductory prognoses that migration from the Islamic Mediterranean countries to Europe will increase rapidly in the near future, it is important to develop a restrictive policy oriented toward the labor market. This then must be linked to a concept for cultural integration. Every unemployed Muslim immigrant is susceptible to fundamentalism. It will be hard to make this kind of immigrant understand that the labor market and not some kind of "crusader mentality" (*al-salibbya*) is the cause of his economic condition. For this reason the policy must be accompanied by hard thinking about the dangers of religious-influenced politicization of the economic (unemployment) and cultural problems of Muslim immigrants. There exists a triangle: the Islamic diaspora community, the community based on country of origin, and naturally the European host country. This triangular connection is loaded with potential conflict that must be defused. Islamic nations have no interest in having Europe offering logistics to the fundamentalist underground.

The needed European policies of immigration and integration should be specially tailored to master the conflict potential of the cited triangular connection. They should also include attempts to strengthen Islamic reform efforts among the Muslims living in Europe as well as attempts to prevent fundamentalist forces from using democracy to assert their fundamentalist ghetto-Islam against reformist Euro-Islam. Allowing a predominance of ghetto-Islam would mean increasing the potential for conflict, not defusing it by integration. I must repeat: Every Muslim immigrant who is not culturally and economically integrated (in the labor market) is susceptible to the Islamic ghetto of an anti-Western-oriented collective. In this context Gilles Kepel speaks of "les balieus d'islam" (see note 23). At the present Islamic fundamentalists are misusing democracy to direct their political activities in the Arabic Mediterranean countries from the European capitals. After the terrorist attack on the World Trade Center in New York, in which parts of the Muslim community in Germany were involved, the Egyptian president Mubarak called upon the West to cooperate with the Muslim countries against fundamentalism.[26]

Only a Euro-Islam that is depoliticized, tolerant, and liberal can be integrated in Europe. This cultural precondition must be coupled with economic and social integration of the people in question—but this will only be possible when European governments only allow as many immigrants as the labor market can tolerate. In clear words this means a quantitatively and qualitatively very restrictive immigration policy. It is also necessary to put an end to using the right to political asylum as a back door to immigration. Every crisis in the European economy that endangers the integration of Muslim immigrants contains the danger that it will drive these people into the hands of the fundamentalist representatives of ghetto-Islam. In contrast to those who are socially and economically incorporated in society, immigrants who cannot be economically integrated can also not be absorbed into democratic political culture. Thus they will remain a potential danger for democracy. Political Islam finds its sustenance in situations of economic hardship.

If we keep in mind that the sketched triangle is also a north-south conflict such as is taking shape in the Mediterranean, then we can recognize that conflicts with ghetto-Islam in Europe can expand to become perilous conflicts in the Mediterranean area itself. Only a liberal, tolerant Islam can diminish German fears of the alien and thus also of Muslims. Calls by Islamic fundamentalists to apply the Sharia even in secular Germany can only lead to reinforcing already present xenophobia.

Promoting Euro-Islam in Europe means helping the development of a third, liberal and tolerant and thus democratically integrated religious community, but not playing the game of a multicultural society, which would mean nothing less than a multiethnic focal point of conflict. In this context we must consider the question about the naturalization process as a means of integration. Europeans should rely on the norm of individual citizenship in the sense of *citoyenneté* (and thus *ius soli*), not resort to notions of collective group membership in the sense of *ius sanguinis*. I also consider double citizenship extremely problematic for Muslims. In contrast to French citizenship law, which is based in *ius soli*, German law is tailored to *ius sanguinis*. Germany grants citizenship to any ethnic German, even to those whose ancestors were once German and who today do not even speak broken German, while the Turks who were born in Germany and who are at home here are denied this right. This criticism is also aimed at transferring *ius sanguinis* to immigrants from the Mediterranean area, which would have devastating consequences for Europe.

Belonging to an ethnic-religious group as a form of a collective should in a democracy not be given greater weight than individual citizenship. *Citoyenneté* is individual membership in a democratic community, not in a collective. For Euro-Muslims, acquisition of European citizenship should be linked to expected identification with and loyalty to a democratic community and not be seen as a convenient way to acquire rights. Integration is not a one-way street. Not only the European nations have to fulfill the task of developing a political concept like this. The Muslims who live in Europe should also be given the task of working on a Euro-Islam that would permit them to feel at home as democratic citizens in Europe. In this way Muslims integrated according to the definitions of the Basic Law could—if they so desire—serve as models of liberal Islam against the totalitarian misuse of Islam by fundamentalism.[27] Fundamentalists consider the Islamic community in Germany and in Europe to be a component of the Daar al-Islam, or "House of Islam," and are, like German right-wing radicals, opposed to integrating the Muslims living in Germany into a democratic community. In *Islamische Minderheiten in der Welt*, a book that appeared in Cairo, one can read on page 172 that communism, "crusadism," and Zionism are engaged in a conspiracy against the Muslims in Europe and desire to use integration to "liquidate the Islamic presence." On page 176 one can read: "In France the crusader mentality that desires to Christianize Muslims is still very much alive.... Zionism ... and the Bahai religion are also playing along here in an attempt to liquidate the Islamic presence in France."[28] Enlightening these antidemocratic tendencies opposed to integration policies can only succeed if they are linked to a practical warning against using such trends to make Islam a hostile image (see note 25). Like Germany, France is a secular country in which integration is not the same as "Christianization!" Anti-Semitism and xenophobia share their tendency of viewing Jews and foreigners as an "alien presence" and rejecting their integration. But one can only integrate people who are willing to enter into that kind of relationship. Fundamentalists vehemently reject the integration of the Islamic community in Europe according to the precepts of European culture.

3. FACIT

Anti-Semitism and xenophobia have only two things in common: They stand in the way of establishing democracy in Germany, and their psychosocial and political attitudes give expression to the authoritarian German personality with its rejection of all that is alien and its aggressive, antidemocratic attitudes. Beyond these two things that they share, foreigners and Jews, victims of xenophobia and anti-Semitism, offer no other criteria that would justify comparing or equating the two groups.

Among the foreigners there is, however, a differentiated group of Muslims (in neither a religious nor a cultural sense is there such a thing as an Islamic bloc) who represent themselves as a collective and want to be recognized by the Germans as such and who desire to be seen by the German public as a collective. Herein lie the problems that can lead to forming Islamic ghettos; this challenge can only be mastered by democratically integrating Muslims into the political community. For this option I have coined the term "Euro-Islam." It would be fatal for German democracy if it—intended or not—promoted this trend to ghetto-Islam and if it were to make concessions to premodern cultures under the guise of being kind to foreigners and in the context of granting rights to cultural collectives. Most immigrants from the Mediterranean are members of premodern cultures, such that a conflict could arise between modern and premodern norms, values, and worldviews; this could exacerbate already existing xenophobia. Permitting undemocratic traditions and customs from premodern cultures to exist in a democratic society would mean not only undermining democracy but also misunderstanding tolerance. Islamic fundamentalists, who like to avail themselves of the opportunities offered by European democracy, recently, in the Turkish city of Sivas, burned alive thirty-five Muslim writers who had displayed secular tendencies.[29] There is no place in Europe for this kind of barbarism and intolerance. Tolerance does not mean being passive about democratic norms and values.

The dialogue between liberal and democratic Islam and the enlightenment about the totalitarian character of Islamic fundamentalism should in Germany and Europe be viewed as part of a general problem-solving strategy. A democratic Germany and Euro-Islam could then establish a relationship of symbiotic tolerance if both were willing to reject right-wing radicalism in the form of xenophobia and fundamentalism.[30]

NOTES

1. Georg Lukacs, *Die Zerstörung der Vernunft* (Neuwied, 1992), 37–83.
2. Bassam Tibi, "Falsche Parallele. Antisemitismus und Ausländerfeindlichkeit," *Frankfurter allgemeine Zeitung* (15 April 1993): 12.
3. The concept of cultural modernism that I have used in my books about Islamic fundamentalism and in this paper is heavily indebted to Jürgen Habermas's *Der philosophische Diskurs der Moderne* (Frankfurt, 1985).
4. Here I am thinking of *Reden an die deutsche Nation*, the demagogic writing of the late Fichte that found considerable resonance with anti-Western Arab nationalists. For more on the influence of German romanticism on Arabic nationalism, see the Fichte chapter in Bassam Tibi, *Vom Gottesreich zum Nationalstaat. Islam und panarabischer Nationalismus*, 3rd expanded ed. (Frankfurt, 1991), 116ff. This book is a part of my Islam trilogy. The other volumes are *Der Islam und das Problem der kulturellen Bewältigung sozialen Wandels* (Frankfurt, 1993) and *Die Krise des modernen Islam*, fourth printing of the expanded Suhrkamp edition (Frankfurt, 1991).
5. Bassam Tibi, "Nicht über Bagdad, sondern direkt! Die Schwierigkeit, an der deutschen Universität heimisch zu sein," *Fremd in einem alten Land. Ausländer in Deutschland* ed. Namo Aziz (Freiburg, 1992), 121–36.
6. Bassam Tibi, "Was denken die Deutschen," *BMW-Dokumentation des Symposiums "Denk' ich an Deutschland,"* organized by the BMW-Quandt-Stiftung at the Church of St. Paul in Frankfurt, 26 April 1991 (Munich, 1991).
7. Shlomo Avineri, *Hegels Theorie des modernen Staates* (Frankfurt, 1976).
8. Reinhard Bendix, *Von Berlin nach Berkeley* (Frankfurt, 1985), contains the story of a German Jew and his identification problems that also has validity for German foreigners.
9. Michael Wolffsohn, *Keine Angst vor Deutschland* (Erlangen, 1990).
10. See note 6.
11. *Rassismus in Europa*, ed. Christoph Butterwegge and Siegfried Jäger (Cologne, 1992), BDG-Bud-Verlag's collection of essays, seems to me to contain such a "high-minded" tone. Wolfgang Kowalsky, in his review "Gesinnungsstark," correctly noted that this kind of argumentation contains the danger of departing from civic, legal, and constitutional principles and ending up in an antiracist dictatorship, *Frankfurter allgemeine Zeitung* (4 May 1993).
12. In the Federal Republic we hardly recognize the problems of ethnicity. In some cases this is confused with "racism" because of a lack of knowledge. (See note 11.) In the United States the connection between immigration and ethnicity is being discussed with great concern. See the report from the United States in Bassam Tibi, "Wird Amerika libanisiert? Die öffentliche Diskussion über Migration in einem Einwanderungsland," *Frankfurter allgemeine Zeitung* (23 May 1992): 12. Key works about ethnicity are Donald Horowitz, *Ethnic Groups in Conflict* (Berkeley, 1985), and Anthony D. Smith, *The Ethnic Origins of Nations* (Oxford, 1986). Recently Daniel Patrick Moynihan's *Pandaemonium: Ethnicity and International Politics* (Oxford and New York, 1993) caused much excitement.

13. Bassam Tibi, "Zum Schaden integrierter Ausländer," *Frankfurter allgemeine Zeitung* (18 December 1992): 13.
14. Max Horkheimer, *Kritische Theorie,* 2 vols. (Frankfurt, 1968), 1:xiii.
15. Helmuth Plessner, *Diesseits der Utopie* (Frankfurt, 1976), 9.
16. Among the best works on anti-Semitism is the essay collection of my Jewish friend and colleague Maxime Rodenson, *Peuple juif ou probleme juif?* (Paris, 1981).
17. See the German edition of Adorno's *Studien zum autoritären Charakter* (Frankfurt, 1973) that was originally published in the United States during the emigration years.
18. Abraham Leon, *Judenfrage und Kapitalismus* (Munich, 1991).
19. See Thomas von Münchhausen's editorial "Frankreich korrigiert alte Fehler," *Frankfurter allgemeine Zeitung* (3 July 1993) and J. von Uthmann, "Einwanderung und wie man damit umgeht," *Frankfurter allgemeine Zeitung* (26 June 1993), on the situation in the United States.
20. See the report about the third conference of the Mediterranean regions by Sybille Quennet, "Die Europäer fürchten die Zuwanderung aus Nordafrika," *Frankfurter allgemeine Zeitung* (27 April 1993). The conference took place in Taormina, Sicily, a traditional location of European-Islamic interchange.
21. See Bassam Tibi, "Immer noch Wind in den Segeln. Der islamische Fundamentalismus nach dem Golfkrieg," *Frankfurter allgemeine Zeitung* (6 February 1992).
22. Repeatedly stressing that the ancient religion of Islam must not be confused with recent fundamentalism (cf. note 25) is no protection from being accused of "racism." In my widely read essay on this topic, "Bedroht uns der Islam?" that appeared in *Der Spiegel* 5 (1993) I expressly warned of identifying Islam with fundamentalism. On fundamentalism see B. Tibi, *Die fundamentalistische Herausforderung. Der Islam und die Weltpolitik* (Munich, 1993), and idem, *Islamischer Fundamentalismus, moderne Wissenschaft und Technologie* (Frankfurt, 1992).
23. On the Muslims of France see Gilles Kepel, *Les Banlieues de l'Islam. Naissance d'une religion en France* (Paris, 1987). On Muslims in western Europe see Thomas Gerholm and Y. Georg Lithman, eds., *The New Islamic Presence in Western Europe* (London, 1988).
24. Bassam Tibi, "Euro-Islam oder Ghetto-Islam. Muslimische Einwanderer und Integration in den EG-Ländern," *Frankfurter allgemeine Zeitung* (7 December 1992): 14, and from the same author, "Euro-Muslime als Brücke zwischen Orient und Okzident?" *Das Parlament* (8–15 January 1993): 11 (a special focus issue of this magazine on foreigners in Germany).
25. See the polemical denunciation of my democratic concept of "Euro-Islam" in the *Tageszeiting* article "Nur ein Euro-Muslim ist ein guter Muslim" (6 March 1993).
26. See Khalid Duran, "An den Türmen von Babylon. Hintergründe des Anschlags auf das World Trade Center in New York," *Frankfurter allgemeine Zeitung* (6 April 1993): 12–13; and *International Herald Tribune* (31 March 1993).
27. Conspiracies are part of the thinking of fundamentalism; fundamentalists who live in Europe impute that there is a Western crusade against the world of Islam; these people are in the way of a better understanding between the Orient and the Occident. See Bassam Tibi, *Die Verschwörung. Das Trauma arabischer Politik* (Hamburg, 1993), esp. chapter 5, pp. 132ff; and part 4, pp. 273ff.

28. Muhammad Abdullah Al-Samman, *Mihnatal-aqaliyyatal-Muslima fi al-'Alam* (Cairo, 1987).
29. See Wolfgang Günter Lerch, "Stadt der toten Dichter. Die Fundamentalisten von Sivas," *Frankfurter allgemeine Zeitung* (6 July 1993).
30. See B. Tibi, "Deutsche Ausländerfeindlichkeit-ethnisch-religiöser Rechtsradikalismus der Ausländer, zwei Gefahren für die Demokratie," *Gewerkschaftliche Monatshefte* (August 1993): 493–502.

CONTRIBUTORS

JULIUS H. SCHOEPS. Born in Djursholm, Sweden, in 1942. Studied history, politics, communications, and theater in Erlangen and Berlin. Ph.D. 1969. Habilitation 1973. 1974–92, professor of political science at the University of Duisburg. In 1986 he founded the Salomon Ludwig Sternheim Institute for German-Jewish History. Since 1992, professor of modern history and director of the Moses Mendelssohn Center for European-Jewish Studies at the University of Potsdam. Since 1993, also founding director of the Jewish Museum of the city of Vienna.

PETER LONGERICH. Born in 1955 in Krefeld. Ph.D. 1984–89, member of the Institute for Recent History in Munich. Since 1993 lecturer at the Royal Holloway College of the University of London. Numerous publications, among them *The Brown Battalions* (1989), *The Files of the Party Chancellery* (1990), *The Murder of the European Jews* (ed., 1988).

ERNST PIPER. Born in 1952 in Munich. Studied medieval history, modern history, and philosophy in Munich and Berlin. Ph.D. 1981; dissertation, *Der Stadtplan als Grundriß der Gesellschaft. Topographie und Sozialstruktur in Augsburg und Florenz*. Managing partner of the publishing house Piper Verlag and journalistic publications. Most important publications: *Der Aufstand der Ciompi. Über den Tumult, den die Wollarbeiter im Florenz der Frührenaissance anzettelten* (1978); *Savonarola. Umtriebe eines Politikers und Puritaners im Florenz der Medici* (1979); *Ernst Barlach und die nationalsozialistische Kunstpolitik* (1982); *Historikerstreit. Die Kontroverse um die Einzigartigkeit der Judenvernichtung* (ed., 1987); *Historikerstreit: The Original Documents. The Recent Controversy in Germany Concerning the National Socialist Annihilation of the Jews* (Atlantic Highlands, NJ: Humanities Press, 1993); *München. Die Gesichte einer Stadt* (with R. Bauer, 1992).

OTTO SCHILY. Born in 1937 in Bochum. Studied law in Munich, Hamburg, and Berlin. Known as a defense lawyer in many large trials, including the Red Army Faction trials. Since 1983 (with interruptions), member of the Bundestag, first with the Greens, then, since 1990, with the SPD.

THOMAS SCHMID. Born in 1945 in Leipzig. Studied German in Frankfurt. Student movement. Later editor with various newspapers (among them *Der Freibeuter*). Several years as an editor at a publishing house, then as a free-lance writer and advisor to the Office for Multicultural Affairs in Frankfurt. Currently heads the culture department at the newspaper *Wochenpost*. Last major publication: *Heimat Babylon. Das Wagnis der multikulturellen Demokratie* (1992).

BASSAM TIBI. Born in 1944 in Damascus. Professor of international politics at Göttingen since 1973, and parallel appointment at Harvard since 1988. Research in most Arabic countries and guest professorships in the United States, Asia, and Africa. Most recent publications include *Conflict Region Middle East* (1992), *The Fundamentalist Challenge* (1992), and *The Conspiracy* (1993).

INDEX

Willstätter, Richard, 39
Wirtschaftspartei [Economics Party],
  31
Wirtschaftswunder [economic miracle],
  vii, 57
Wolffsohn, Michael, 89
working class, in Weimar Republic, 30
Würzburg Workers Council, 53

xenophobia, 69, 74, 75, 77, 78, 79, 82,
  85–102

Yalta agreement, 77
Yilmaz, Ayse, 75
Young Plan, 26

Zelinsky, Hartmut, 8, 9